HAUNTED
CARLISLE

Carlisle Cathedral.

HAUNTED CARLISLE

Darren W. Ritson

The
History
Press

To the good folk of Carlisle.

First published 2012

The History Press
The Mill, Brimscombe Port
Stroud, Gloucestershire, GL5 2QG
www.thehistorypress.co.uk

© Darren W. Ritson, 2012

The right of Darren W. Ritson to be identified as the Author
of this work has been asserted in accordance with the
Copyrights, Designs and Patents Act 1988.

British Library Cataloguing in Publication Data.
A catalogue record for this book is available from the British Library.

ISBN 978 0 7524 6087 1

Typesetting and origination by The History Press
Printed in Great Britain

Contents

Acknowledgements

FIRSTLY, I would like to thank paranormal historian, Paul Adams – co-author of *The Borley Rectory Companion*, and renowned expert on the life and times of the great psychical researcher Harry Price (1881–1948) – for penning the foreword to this book. I would also like to thank the good people of Carlisle for being so warm, friendly and, most of all, keen to share their stories for this book on the ghosts of Carlisle. Thanks to Carlisle resident, David Harkins, for sharing his ghost stories with me and for the use of two images produced herein. Thanks must also go to the *Cumberland News*, namely Sue Crawford and Meg Jorsh, for publishing a story about the writing of this very book. Massive thanks must go to my good friend Mike Hallowell, for his usual on-going support and assistance during the compilation of this book. To my trusty North East Ghost Research Team member and old psychic pal Suzanne Hitchinson, for pointing me in the direction of some fascinating tales of ghosts. To Jan Mayer, owner of the Dalston Hall Hotel, for sharing his amazing stories with me; your co-operation was most welcomed and your kindness most appreciated. Thanks to Maggie McClellan and the staff from the Crown and Mitre Hotel, for their hospitality and their kindness during my visits there.

My thanks go to Dr Simon Sherwood of Northampton University, for his advice and information regarding the 'black dog'. Thanks must also go to Syd Whitehead (Hon. Secretary of the Marie Stuart Society), for his advice regarding the Queen of Scotland's sojourns during her captivity at Carlisle Castle. Thanks to Stuart Davison and Sue Howarth from Carlisle railway station for their help and support during the compilation of this book; thanks too for allowing me to spend many nights at the station, in search of its ghosts. My thanks go to Dougie Kerr and Dave Maclachlan from the Carlisle Laser Quest, for their testimonies and assistance during my research for this book, and Mark of the Brickyard music venue, Sam Kane and James Heasley for telling me their accounts of the strange happenings therein. I offer my thanks to Julie Olley and Drew Bartley, who kindly produced illustrations for inclusion in this book. Finally, thanks to everyone else that I have spoken to and helped me along the way – you know who you are.

Also by the Author

Ghosts at Christmas
Haunted Berwick
Haunted Durham
Haunted Newcastle
Haunted Northumberland
Haunted Tyneside
The Haunting of Willington Mill: The Truth Behind England's Most Enigmatic Ghost Story
(With Michael J. Hallowell)
The South Shields Poltergeist: One Family's Fight against an Invisible Intruder
(With Michael J. Hallowell)

Foreword

'DO you believe in ghosts?' is a familiar and frequently asked question. The author of this book, Darren W. Ritson, does, and he has spent many years of study, research and practical investigation in order to provide the proof to support his convictions. It must be said that the serious investigation of the paranormal is an undertaking not to be given superficial attention, demanding as it does a commitment to the examination and understanding of a strange, unpredictable and mysterious subject. It is, however, a subject for which convincing evidence exists, for a wide range of curious and intriguing phenomena stretching back over hundreds of years has been reported and recorded by human communities and civilisations across the entire world; it includes the appearance of apparitions, the existence of haunted houses and buildings, poltergeist infestations, the psychic dimension of mediumship and channelling, as well as prophetic dreams and time-slips. The interaction between the world of the unseen and that of mankind has created world religions, defies currently accepted scientific thinking, and continues to provoke and fascinate; and a major factor in this continued interest in the supernatural realm is the world of ghosts and haunted places.

The task of the objective ghost hunter involves a number of disparate and time-consuming activities. As well as historical research, interviewing witnesses to paranormal phenomena, assessing the validity of the claimants' experiences, and visiting allegedly haunted locations, for many researchers – and Darren in particular – carrying out investigative vigils and the employment of technical equipment in obtaining evidence of ghostly activity, is of paramount importance. In *Haunted Carlisle*, paranormalist Darren continues his survey of supernormal phenomena, mainly in the North of England, which to date has taken place in his home town of Newcastle-upon-Tyne,

The road sign welcoming people to Carlisle.

At some point in the future, perhaps a lifetime away, maybe more, mankind will have the answers to the elusive reality of the paranormal world that is seemingly all around us. Since what could be described as the 'occult revolution' in twentieth century Britain, which has steadily gathered momentum from its initial beginnings in the 1960s, the growing public interest and acceptance of ghostly phenomena has resulted in an increased and detailed chronicling of Britain's strange and haunted places, and the present volume admirably continues this tradition. Carlisle and its neighbouring regions are known for several high-profile supernatural cases, most notably the 'Radiant Boy' phantom of Corby Castle. The city itself boasts a number of paranormal sites – the cathedral, the castle, the railway station and several public houses, are all haunted places and the author has visited them personally, along with many others, to compile the records of strange, thought-provoking and eerie happenings which, through these pages, you will soon be encountering for yourself.

So, join your guide, Darren W. Ritson, for a ghostly tour of haunted Carlisle – to be enjoyed with the lights low, if you dare…

Paul Adams
Bedfordshire, 2012

together with neighbouring Durham city, Berwick-upon-Tweed, along with the counties of Tyneside, Wearside, County Durham and Northumberland, as well as many other places across the UK. This has involved a combination of desktop study, practical investigation and personal experiences – a successful combination that has, again, produced another comprehensive and entertaining volume of ghostly activity.

Introduction

AFTER penning a number of books, including *Haunted Newcastle, Haunted Durham, Haunted Berwick, Haunted Tyneside* and *Haunted Northumberland*, I decided that it was time to make the journey across the top of northern England and explore the haunted heritage of Carlisle, in the North West. Carlisle is a very historical place indeed, with its own abundance of social, architectural and cultural enigmas. It also has customs, traditions and many wonderful visual reminders of yesteryear in almost every place you choose to look. These are some of the main reasons why I was drawn here; to investigate its fascinating, and in a way exceptional, history, whether it *is* paranormal, or not. Of course, it goes without saying that the paranormal aspect of my research is what this book is largely composed of.

The Roman's settled here over 2,000 years ago, with their base being established to serve the forts along Hadrian's Wall. Known as *Luguvalium*, Carlisle is situated only ten miles from the Scottish border. Because of its close proximity to Scotland, during the Middle Ages it became an important military stronghold. Carlisle is the largest settlement in the county of Cumbria, and much like Berwick-upon-Tweed, it has been fought over many times and has belonged to *both* the English and Scottish empires. This was of course before these two countries became part of the United Kingdom. Interestingly, Carlisle does not appear in the Domesday Book, simply because at that particular time in history, when the book was created, Carlisle was in the hands of the Scots.

The historic city of Carlisle is the gateway to the magnificent Lake District in Cumbria. It is a direct link to the North West, and is a city with much charm, character and allure. Lying approximately fifty miles from the walled city of Newcastle-upon-Tyne, Carlisle is one of two cities that the magnificent Roman structure known as Hadrian's Wall runs through; my native Newcastle-upon-Tyne, of course, being the second.

A stone engraving of Carlisle's old coat of arms. The coat of arms has now been updated but the motto remains the same: Be Just and Fear Not.

Being an ancient and historical metropolis, it is not surprising that the city of Carlisle and its outskirts are brimming with wonderful folkloric tales, romantic ghostly anecdotes, and spine-chilling incidences that would most certainly give you goosebumps and send your flesh creeping. What is puzzling, however, is the lack of *collected* anecdotes, or books for that matter, that detail these stories of spectres and phantoms. I would have thought there were many books dedicated to Carlisle's residents ghosts, but I am wrong. Granted, there are many fine books out there that contain ghost stories and harrowing tales of the supernatural from in and around Carlisle, such as Peter Underwood's *Ghosts of the North West*, and Jack Hallam's *Ghosts of the North*, but to the best of my knowledge, at the time of writing there is only one that collects a large quantity of Carlisle's ghost stories in one volume – this one.

Carlisle is a wonderful, old, partially walled town and I always enjoy visiting the city to meander through the old side streets, exploring the stores, shops and attractions that Carlisle has to offer. Being able to visit this great city, solely for the purpose of discovering its ghostly population, has been a task that I have certainly enjoyed. For each and every ghost story discovered and discussed in this book, you can bet your bottom dollar that there will be at least one or two more waiting to be unearthed. Ghosts, it seems, are everywhere, and no matter how many accounts are found within these pages, this book will not do the city of Carlisle any justice – but I have tried.

One of the many 'nooks and crannies' within the beautiful old city of Carlisle.

Carlisle is an ancient, numinous conurbation with its fair share of old side streets, alleyways and nooks and crannies. It has brand-spanking new buildings integrated with the town's edifices; ancient and modern complementing each other perfectly. Remember, one of the most important aspects of a good ghost story is the setting, and you could wish for no better setting than Carlisle when it comes to wraiths, phantasms and other spectral entities of the other world.

Darren W. Ritson, 2012

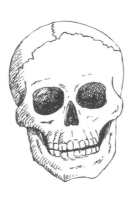

1

The Ghosts of Carlisle

The Citadel Restaurant Ghost of 1966

English Street in Carlisle is host to a once glorious citadel, now a tourist attraction, and is the scene of a haunting that dates back to 1966. The first sighting of the ghost, according to Jack Hallum in his book *Ghosts of the North* (1976), occurred when the spectre appeared to a customer waiting for a friend in the Arcade Bar. This harrowing shade appeared to be around 5ft 7in tall, dark grey in colour, and was said to have walked across the room after emerging through a solid wall. Then, after traversing the room, it just disappeared into the floor as though it was 'poured into the ground'. This occurred only yards from where the astonished customer was sitting.

The customer said that although it had no recognisable features, he 'knew it was a man'. I understood exactly what he meant by this, as I had a similar experience whilst carrying out investigations at the former Prisoner of War camp in Harperley, in County Durham, on the night of 30 July 2005. I had been asked to co-investigate the premises with a north-east based research team, Anomalous Phenomena Investigations (API), when the sighting occurred. I was standing outside of Hut 13, chatting to some colleagues during a break from our night vigils, at 12.30 a.m. During the course of our conversation, I became aware of a figure in my peripheral vision but thought nothing of it, as I surmised it was another investigator having a look round. I continued chatting with my colleagues, however, after a short while, I was still aware that this figure was 'skulking' about.

I now felt compelled to turn and look, to satisfy my curiosity, and was shocked to see that it was not any of my colleagues, but a figure in black (somehow I knew it was a male). I determined this fact when he walked forwards and straight into the back of a farmyard tractor that was parked there. I then watched as the figure vanished into thin air – it just disintegrated before my eyes. The sighting lasted no more than a few seconds, but

Remnants of the old sign from the Citadel Restaurant.

The Citadel Restaurant on English Street, once haunted by an eerie black shadow that disappeared into the floor.

dark in colour. However, my apparition sighting disappeared into thin air while the Citadel Restaurant ghost vanished through the floor. There is something distinctly chilling about the way this apparition made its exit from the restaurant, don't you agree? In fact, I believe that this aspect of the sighting makes it a far more sinister tale than that of the Harperley ghost.

This begs the questions, just what are these apparitions? Why do they appear colourless, or dark? Are they ghosts of the dead, or perhaps something entirely different? Some people suggest that they may be an amalgamation of negative forces, that somehow converts or transforms into an anthropomorphic entity; an entity that has never actually lived as a 'human', so to speak. Normal ghosts (as normal as ghosts can get, anyway) usually disappear in the more orthodox, or accepted, fashion by slowly fading into the ether, or simply vanishing in the blink of an eye, not sinking into the floor in a most unusual way.

Regardless of what occurred in English Street back in 1966, the fact remains that these ghost sightings continue to be reported by credible and trustworthy individuals, who have no

I saw this 'thing' long enough to know that there was something there, and I am confident that it was something otherworldly.

The ghost of the citadel is, in some respects, comparable to my sighting in Durham, in particular to two odd similarities. We both assumed that our apparitions were that of a male, or at least they took the shape of a male, and both entities were either black or very

English Street.

reason whatsoever to make these kinds of stories up. The sighting at the Citadel Restaurant, as far as I am aware, was a one-off, and to the best of my knowledge it has not been reported there again. One wonders if the Harperley Prisoner of War camp ghost has been seen again; after all, it has been over six years since I saw it.

The Ghost of the Sergeant's Father

Here is an interesting tale of a haunting which is recounted in Jack Hallam's book *Ghosts of the North* (1976), but was originally told by a Staffordshire man named Gerald Findler. Findler had lived in Cumbria for forty years and had written a number of books on the Lake District's ghosts and legends. Findler had worked as an orderly in the city's auxiliary hospital during the First World War, and it was during his time there that he had a brush with the paranormal.

A man answering to the name of Sergeant Chase – a sergeant in the Australian Army – had been brought into the makeshift hospital (normally the local school) with horrific wounds to his back.

It turned out he was caught up in an explosion, which resulted in shrapnel and debris tearing open his back and leaving him very seriously injured. Findler and another nurse looked after Sergeant Chase for twenty-four hours of the day, and were completely devoted to his well-being. Since the hospital was an improvised place of care, there were not that many patients there at that time. Had it been a real hospital of course, there would have been hundreds of patients. This meant Findler and the nurse could spend a lot more time devoting their efforts to fewer hospital inmates, which of course would have been ideal for them.

Every night, Findler would tend to the sergeant, who was housed in a small hut in the school playground, and read books to him by lamplight until he drifted off to sleep. Once he fell asleep, Findler would turn out the light and tend to other orderly duties. One night in 1917, as he made his way to see Sergeant Chase, he noticed that the lamp light he used to read with was shining bright through the window. Upon entering the hut, Findler saw an elderly man sitting by the bed of Sergeant Chase, who was holding tightly on to his hand. Findler smiled at the old gentleman, and closed the door. He thought to himself he would come back later after Sergeant Chase's visitor – his father, he assumed – had left.

Upon chatting with the other nurse during a tea-break, he mentioned to her the night-time visitor, to which she replied, 'Never, not at this time of night'. They both put their teacups down and ventured back across to where Sergeant

Graves in Carlisle Cemetery; the body of Sergeant Chase lies somewhere within the confines of this old burial ground.

An artist's representation of Sergeant Chase's grave. (Courtesy of Julie Olley)

Chase was resting, and lo and behold the old gent was still there. After briefly seeing the old man through the window, they made their way inside the hut to find that the lamp light – that had just a few seconds earlier been glowing – had now been extinguished, leaving the room in complete darkness. Upon lighting the lamp they were astonished to find the old man nowhere in sight. There was only one way in and one way out. So, where had he gone? And who was he? Worse still, they were then distressed to realise that their patient, the lovely Sergeant Chase, was lying dead in his bed.

Findler and the nurse laid out the sergeant and carried out their after-death duties with care. Whilst they sorted out his belongings they came across his wallet, in which there was a number of old black and white photographs. You can only imagine what Findler and the nurse felt when they found a photograph of an elderly man; the same elderly man that they had both seen earlier in the hut holding onto Sergeant Chase's hand. It turned out that he *was* Chase's father, but that he had died many, many years previously.

Findler and the nurse attended the funeral of Sergeant Chase one week after his sad death. For whatever reason, his body was not sent home to Australia and was subsequently interred during a military funeral service, which took place at Carlisle Cemetery. The grave, if one looks hard enough, can still be seen, and stands bearing the name 'Sergeant Chase'.

The Devil Dog of Carlisle

Phantom hounds, or devil dogs, are a harrowing aspect of the paranormal. Wherever you live, you are not far from a ghost dog from hell. They roam the UK from one end to the other, in search of their next victim. In fact, if you live near an old graveyard, the chances are it is haunted by such a creature. You see, back in days gone by, local folk, when opening up a new burial ground, would bury alive a big black dog, as tradition had it that the first burial in the cemetery would be destined to come back in spirit and haunt the graveyard for eternity. This ghost was said to roam around, patrolling the area and generally taking care of the graveyard. It was known as the graveyard guardian. Believe it or not, prior to people burying their dogs alive, the first to become graveyard guardians were once humans! I am not sure how they decided who should become the graveyard guardian, but whoever was chosen to be buried alive obviously faced a terrible and painful drawn-out death. The sad thing was that the person destined to die to protect the future of the graveyard was usually a good, law-abiding citizen; after all, they were chosen for that special task. Eventually, it was decided that human sacrifice should be abandoned and a dog was selected as a replacement instead.

Mind you, the graveyard guardian is only one kind of 'ghost dog'; there are said to be many more walking the lanes and old roads of the countryside at night, and sometimes at day. Depending on where you live in the UK, the likelihood is that the name of your local 'hound from hell' will differ from those in other parts of the country. For example, in Staffordshire he is known locally as Padfoot, and in East Anglia (more specifically Norfolk), he is known as Black Shuck, or Old Shuck. In Wales, the black dog is identified as *Gwyllgi*, which translated means 'dog of darkness'. In the Midlands he is known as the Hooter, in Yorkshire he is known as Barguest, and in Scotland, ghost dogs are known as the Muckle Black Tyke. In Cumbria, the local folkloric term for these devil dogs are Capelthwaite, or Cappel.

Although the idea of hounds from hell may sound far-fetched, there are many corroborated reports of such creatures terrorising people, stalking the *terra firma* with their razor-sharp teeth clearly on show, their snarling mouths oozing saliva, and their blood-red eyes glowing like discs in the dark. It is all too easy to ridicule such tales and treat the people that have encountered them with scorn and contempt, but mind where you wander, for one day when you least expect it you may just find yourself coming face-to-face with such a beast (if you do, and manage to survive the attack, please do let me know).

One of Carlisle's black dog tales dates back to the nineteenth century. I was going to call it a well-known tale, but I am not sure just how well-known this tale really is. I presume it is relatively unknown, due to the fact its source dates back to a very old newspaper clipping, making the tale itself well outside of most people's recollections. Therefore, I feel it is my duty to publish the story, in

an effort to not only keep the story alive, but to tell it to a whole new generation.

The following story is taken from my book, *Ghosts at Christmas*. In the nineteenth century, I was told, a blacksmith by the name of John Carter made the decision to depart from his London home and move to Carlisle, where he had the chance of better-paid employment with a job that also had really good prospects. The chance to better his own life and that of his wife seemed too good to miss, but it was a decision he would later come to regret. When the Carter family arrived at Carlisle, a day before Christmas, they rented a coach to take them to a nearby village, where they would live in what sounded like a peaceful and pleasant lodging. They were hoping to be settled into their new home well in time for Yuletide. As the coach, driven by a rather well dressed gentleman in a bowler hat, took off through the countryside, John Carter noticed how incredibly foggy it was becoming.

The fog came in thick and fast, but this didn't seem to bother the driver who, if anything, seemed to have a preference for riding at breakneck speed. At one point the carriage almost careered off the road as it manoeuvred round a very sharp corner, but still the coachman used his whip to drive the horse on ever faster. Carter, very much alarmed at this point, shouted for the driver to slow down.

'Nay sire! I daren't! Should I slow the coach now a bad thing will befall us, and no mistake!'

Carter, not one to be messed with by all accounts, kept shouting at the driver;

An artist's representation of the Carlisle 'devil dog'. (Courtesy of Drew Bartley)

insisting that he slow down. Eventually the man agreed, but told the blacksmith that the result would be upon his own head. Not long after, Carter was horrorified to see a terrible looking dog-like creature racing alongside the carriage. It was a large, black dog and it had evil, glowing eyes and a lolling tongue. Every now and then the hell hound would rear up on its hind legs and paw, with intent, at the carriage door, as if trying to get inside.

'Go faster! Go faster!' cried the terrified blacksmith, as his wife shrieked with fear.

'Do you see now, sire? Do you see why I did not want to slow down the carriage and with it our pace?'

John Carter could see all too clearly and fully understood. Now, instead of going slower, he persuaded the coachman to speed up as much as he could.

Mile after mile the carriage thundered through the Cumbrian countryside and the thick, nauseating fog. On occasions, the spectral dog – for that's what it was – would fall behind, before, only moments later to their horror, it would catch up with them again. Eventually, the coach approached a river, and the driver attempted to guide it over a narrow bridge. Alas, the coach was too wide and became stuck on the bridge, causing the driver to shout, 'Now we're done!' Without hesitation the howling, slobbering dog began to paw at the carriage door with such strength that it was only a matter of time before it shattered. In desperation, the coach driver cracked his whip at the beast, causing it to fall from the bridge into the frozen river.

The coachman, blacksmith and his wife watched in relief as the howling canine spectre was washed away in the ice-cold current. Eventually, the coach was freed from the narrow bridge and continued on its journey. Neither Carter nor his wife ever went near that bridge again, in case they should encounter once more the 'hound from hell'. The driver told the blacksmith and his wife that the phantom dog had roamed the area for generations, and that locals were so frightened of it they were forbidden to mention the beast in public. That is why, of course, he set off on the journey with tremendous speed.

The Carlisle Devil Dog 2

Not being content with having one terrifying legend of a devil dog, or phantom hound, Carlisle has to go one step further and boast of two! There are not many places that can lay claim to having two beasts from hell pacing the streets. Of course, the thought occurs that the two following reports of ghostly black dogs could in actual fact be the same dog; I think this is unlikely, however.

The first tale, as we have just heard, dates back one hundred years or so ago, making it a sort of 'folkloric' account. It is a harrowing tale which evokes fear, dread and the thought of possible death to the individuals involved. This second account however, albeit very short, is relatively new – dating back only five or ten years – and is not so much frightening but eerie, as we shall see.

It involves a Carlisle man who was out early one morning making his way home. He takes up the tale …

> On walking home one foggy morning, a large black wolfhound-type animal crossed a junction on Fuse Hill Street in front of me. It gave me an appraising glance and silently went down an ally. Thinking it was an early morning dog-walker's companion I waited for the human owner, who didn't appear. The legendary 'Black Shuck' is a large black dog which patrols the old city boundary. Many places have these black dog tales and I believe they are more spiritual guardians than ghosts.

Short, but interesting. Notice how this man calls the dog 'Black Shuck'? We have discussed earlier on that Black Shuck is indeed a legendary ghost hound but this name is given to dogs seen in Norfolk, or thereabouts, therefore one wonders if the man who reported seeing this dog is originally from that area. Or, perhaps he was just familiar with the term and decided it could be used in this instance. The fact that he can identify a ghost dog, or at least acknowledge the fact it could have been one, is very interesting. Another interesting thing to note is the man's use of the words 'the legendary "Black Shuck", a large black dog which patrols the old city boundary'. This statement is giving rise to a supposition that there is indeed a ghost dog reputed to haunt this area.

Tales of eerie dogs with glowing eyes are very common indeed, and there are more *bona fide* accounts of phantom black dogs than you may think. Of course, it is

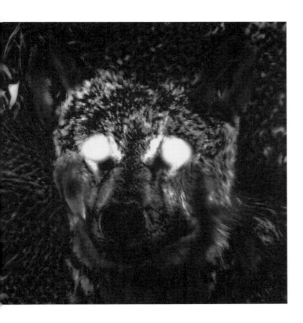

An artist's representation of the second Carlisle 'devil dog' seen near Fuse Hill. (Courtesy of Michael J. Hallowell)

Shields Poltergeist: One Family's Fight Against an Invisible Intruder, and it details the lengthily struggle that an unassuming family in South Tyneside was forced to endure for almost twelve months of their lives. I became involved in the case after the family had tolerated its annoying antics for a few months, and in all honesty I never in a million years dreamed of witnessing what I did. This particular case is special due to its extraordinary length combined with its sheer intensity. Most poltergeist cases can last from one week to a number of years. The Enfield poltergeist of 1977–78 lasted around one and a half years, which, in poltergeist terms is a long time! South Shields lasted almost one year and is one of the reasons why the case received the attention it did.

When a poltergeist manifests in someone's home it can turn their lives upside down and can seriously traumatise those that live in close proximity to it. This happened at both Enfield and South Shields. Fortunately, the Enfield and South Shields cases yielded sufficient data and accumulated dozens of witness testimonies to corroborate what the investigators and the home owners of these cases claimed – that for a designated period of time, an unknown entity or agent generated by a force that is still not understood by mankind, ripped through these houses like a psychic tornado, causing mayhem, abject fear and misery in the process.

easy to take them all with a pinch of salt, but who knows. Hooter; Black Shuck; Padfoot; Barguest; Cappel; whatever he is called, he may be waiting for you the next time you decide to venture out on a dark winter's night.

The Carlisle Poltergeist

Outbreaks of poltergeist activity have been occurring all over the world for many years. No one knows what they are, or indeed how they commit the acts that they do. We do know, however, that they do exist. Indeed, I had the opportunity of investigating a real humdinger of a poltergeist case back in 2006, and – with fellow author and investigator Mike Hallowell – penned an entire account of the whole affair. It is called *The South*

Cases where a great wealth of evidence is collected, documented and observed by investigators are, in many cases, subject to ridicule too. Enfield and South Shields were certainly not exempt from receiving incessant ridicule and ferocious tongue lashings, but at least they stand a better chance of being scrutinised and scientifically verified by those who were/are prepared to keep an open mind. There is no doubt in my mind that cases like Enfield and South Shields (as well as many other well documented cases) go some way to proving the existence of poltergeists; something that the sceptics will have to get to grips with.

The vast majority of poltergeist cases that are encountered never last particularly long (sadly for investigators but happily for their victims), and nine times out of ten they are usually over with before they are even identified as being poltergeists. The activity is at such a low level, that sometimes they are not even detected until they reach their peak, so to speak. By then, they have burnt themselves out. There are also cases that don't last too long but seem to be quite intense and so for a week or two, terror reigns at the site of the activity until it stops, almost as suddenly as it began.

In Carlisle, one such report of a poltergeist outbreak was written up in the papers and made headline news. On 12 September 2007, the *Daily Mail* ran with the headline 'Family flee home after being attacked by poltergeist throwing glasses'. This intrigued me somewhat as it was after Mike and I had investigated the South Shields case, but before the book detailing our findings was released. It has been suggested that certain activity which occurred at the house in Carlisle eerily mirrored some of the phenomenon that was experienced at South Shields, therefore conclusions were drawn that it was a potential hoax or trick in an attempt by the occupants to be re-housed. I am not sure about this conclusion, although to be honest I cannot say anything in regards to it, because I did not witness any of the 'paranormal' activity.

In fact, Guy Lyon Playfair – one of the lead investigators in the famous Enfield Poltergeist case – called me and brought this case to my attention. He had seen it in the paper and thought it may be of interest to me, as I live only a few hours away. He told me that he 'thought it sounded like an interesting case, and like all cases of poltergeist reports, they need looking into'. The case did indeed rouse my interest, but unfortunately any enquiries to the relevant housing authorities yielded no results. I had offered my services to help the family and look into the paranormal activity but, alas, no one got in touch. It was inevitable that other researchers would also offer their services, which was indeed the case in this situation.

The occurrences began at the home of Allison Marshall, who lived in the Raffles area of the city, on Thursday, 30 August 2007, when she and her family were in the house. She had lived in this particular home for four years and had, up until that point, reported nothing at all pertaining to the paranormal. It was a very happy household by all accounts, and it was a home that she and her family loved. Her mother lived just down the road which, for her, was a godsend as she could call upon her whenever she needed help with her four children.

The paranormal activity that occurred on that first night caused everyone to sit up all night, as they were too frightened to go to bed. During the course of the night, the householders witnessed a vast array of bewildering phenomena which, oddly, seemed to come on the hour, or on the half hour. Between 2 a.m. and 4 a.m. the activity intensified, commencing with the dog's bone and a hair brush allegedly flying across the room without anyone touching them. Then, at 3 a.m., a glass that had been placed inside a cabinet somehow flew across the room and hit Allison on the back. Half an hour later, another glass flew off one of the shelves in the house and hit the ceiling fan so hard that it left a dent in the ceiling. At 4 a.m. another glass flew out of the living room and into the hallway wall with such speed that it cracked all the plasterwork; oddly, it seems these glasses remained intact.

By this time Allison and her family were so afraid that she decided to leave the house with her children and sleep at her mother's house. For the next four days and nights, the paranormal activity at the house continued, which left the family bewildered and at a loss in regards with what to do. Allison was too scared to return to the 'haunted house', especially with her four children, saying that it was 'too much of an uncomfortable thought to go back at night'. When asked what she thought was happening, she said that she would 'have to put it down to a poltergeist as there was no other explanation'.

In the space of one week, numerous phenomenon were witnessed in the house, including reports of household objects, such as ornaments and the aforementioned glasses, flying around the living room as though thrown by unseen hands; strange and harrowing noises were heard, including the sound of a baby crying, along with the classical poltergeist bangs and raps; temperature drops; objects being found moved from their original positions and, strangest of all, the image of a human skull was allegedly seen in the window of a glass cabinet. After what Allison had seen at her house in the space of that terrifying

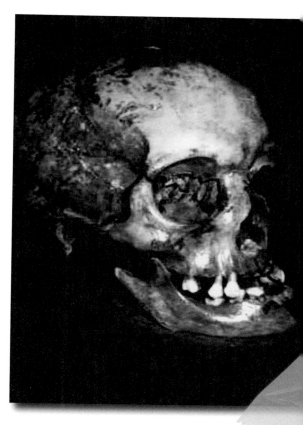

A real human skull encased in glass; the image of a human skull was allegedly seen in the window of a glass cabinet during the Carlisle poltergeist case. (Photograph courtesy of Ian Lodge.)

week, she was quoted as saying that she would probably never return home. Even her next-door neighbour witnessed some of the odd activity going on in the house and concluded that it was most certainly paranormal, although he found it hard to believe at first.

This brief but relatively intense infestation, if it is true, seems to bare the hallmarks of a very short-lived poltergeist. Allison was correct in her diagnosis, I feel, when she suggested that it was a poltergeist. She was unlucky to have gone through this turmoil, but looking back to the South Shields case, she was more than lucky. The occupants of the house in South Shields had to put up with similar, if not worse activity for almost twelve months before they could live in peace again; the Enfield poltergeist was even longer! When it comes to deciding if the case of the Carlisle poltergeist is genuine or not, we can only look at the evidence and the witness testimonies and decide from that. Since I was not there I cannot say for sure, although I can testify to the reality of the phenomenon. I would have loved to have experienced this case but unfortunately it was not to be. A group from Scotland came down to investigate the case for Allison and identified the poltergeist as the ghost of a former neighbour. After an alleged cleansing ceremony, the poltergeist was reported to have left the family in peace.

Carlisle Castle

We now visit the magnificent bastion that is Carlisle Castle. In my opinion, no self-respecting aficionado of the paranormal would visit this fine city without making a beeline for the castle.

Being a member of English Heritage, access to the castle for me is free of charge so every time I come to Carlisle, a trip there is a must.

The beauty of the castle being cared for by English Heritage is the fact that its history is rather easy to research. In Carlisle Castle's case, there are placards and signs posted all over the castle, so whatever room you choose to visit you can guarantee there will be some interesting details to read there. After gleaning some fascinating and detailed history regarding the castle via these handy signs, and chatting with a castle guide, I managed to ascertain some good information.

The castle is a very imposing landmark and dominates the whole area. It has a tumultuous and troubled past, with its 900-year history bearing witness to countless sieges and conflicts. It is thought that the castle stands on the site of an earlier fortification – an earth-and-timber construction. Built by King William Rufus around the year 1100, the castle stood for 100 years before being rebuilt by Henry I. It's towering stone keep, which dominates the complex, is said to be the oldest surviving edifice belonging to this particular establishment.

Inside the castle there is a designated area that was once used as a prison. It is thought that this small holding room was once crammed with people, all living in squalid and disgusting conditions after committing crimes ranging from petty theft to murder. Carvings on the wall still

Carlisle Castle: Mary, Queen of Scots' first English prison, and also the place where a terrifying spectre dressed in old tartan was witnessed.

exist and are said to have been etched into the stone by the detainees of Richard III, in the 1400s. From May to July 1568, in a tower that once stood in the corner of the castle's complex, Mary, Queen of Scots was held as a prisoner. This part of the castle, the 'Queen Mary Tower' as it was known, unfortunately no longer exists. Remnants of its former existence can still be observed in the interior of the grounds if you look close enough.

In 1645, Carlisle Castle was laid siege to for almost ten months during the English Civil War. It's Royalist garrison, it is said, admitted defeat after being forced to eat rats for a number of weeks.

Mary, Queen of Scots.

The corner of Carlisle Castle that once imprisoned Mary, Queen of Scots. Unfortunately now gone, one can only imagine what the tower prison may have looked like.

There is so much to do at Carlisle Castle. When I go, after spending a good deal of time in the great keep, I usually visit the Border Regiment Museum. It is situated inside the inner ward of the castle and relates, in great detail, the history of Cumbria's County Infantry Regiment, from 1702 to the present day. Having visited the museum on many occasions I am compelled to say in all truthfulness, that it is an outstanding display of military artifacts that ranges from cannons to swords, to old rifles to uniforms and other types of armory.

On the top floor of the keep there is a brilliant exhibition on Charles Edward Stuart, who was otherwise known as Bonnie Prince Charlie. It also delves into the 1745 Jacobite Rebellion, and in the centre of the floor, stands a magnificent wooden model of Carlisle and its castle. This in itself is worth the visit alone. A trip to the castle is not complete, however, until you see

Bonnie Prince Charlie.

the infamous 'licking stones' that the mistreated inmates would have been forced to lick and suck on in an attempt to hydrate themselves. Water droplets would seep from the damp walls, and, over time, it would gather in the grooves of the stonework. Fights amongst the dehydrated prisoners would, quite often, break out and be rather brutal as this was the only source of water they would get. This natural act still occurs, so the next time you explore the castle, do have a look to see if any water droplets have accumulated in the small grooves.

In regards to the castle's ghosts, I am aware of only one. This account is detailed in Jack Hallum's book, *Ghosts of the North*. In it he states that many years ago, the skeleton of a woman was found walled up in the keep. No one knows who she was, or why she may have been walled up there. She was, he says, dressed in a faded tartan and had expensive jewellry on. Hallum goes on to say that a sentry guard on duty there had seen the mysterious lady and when he challenged her, she suddenly evaporated into thin air – disappearing without a trace. He is said to have died of shock only a few hours after his encounter. Luckily, he managed to tell his amazing story to his comrades before he slipped off in to the next world.

I must now tell you about one psychic medium (who wishes to remain anonymous) that I have spent many a night with in haunted locations. This medium, who has been labelled as 'the UK exorcist', once spent the night in Carlisle Castle in his quest for searching out ghosts. I might add, that to the best of my knowledge, this was the one and only occasion when Carlisle Castle opened its doors to ghost hunters, so I couldn't resist catching up with him to find out just what happened during the investigation.

'It was a real honour that was bestowed upon me, allowed to roam free into the areas of unspoken truths', he told me.

I then enquired about what he sensed and picked up on throughout the examination of the castle. He said:

> The first place I walked into I was told [by spirits] of a death and a coffin within these rooms and I have to respect the man. I was then led to two empty rooms where I explained in detail the uses for each room; I was proved correct by the guides and historians that were attending with me. One was for a prisoner called 'Major' and the other was used for a coffin that belonged to royalty. I then picked up on a spirit man that looked down on everyone and described them as peasants. After describing the man I mentioned the name James I, but I thought 'No, it can't be'. At this point one of the attending guides said, 'You have just described him and why he is here'.

I then asked the medium what else he experienced whilst at the castle, and he told me that:

> The cellars revealed more than anyone was expecting, as names were very much forthcoming and many disembodied voices were heard by all present. I explained that it felt like there were many people packed in the room like animals, to be informed later on that 341 men were confined in this area of the castle. They were to be hanged, drawn and quartered, and the terror, pain and anguish that I could clearly sense from these men, was firmly embedded into the fabric of this atmosphere and these walls, never to leave.

After he had regaled his tales, I proceeded to ask him how he felt the night had gone, to which he replied:

> The night proved rather interesting as we recorded some unusual facts. There were *some* incidents that are worth mentioning that occurred during our vigils in there. Unexplained footfalls or tapping noises that could have been described as footfalls were heard by me, and a number of individuals in the 'prison room' at the foot of the keep. We also heard this weird humming noise! The odd thing was, was that every time I mentioned this spirit I had sensed, called Tom … we heard this strange noise. It was really strange. We all also heard a cat 'meowing' when there was no cat on site! It was a really good, but strange night. We were the first group, incidentally, ever to be allowed into Carlisle Castle to investigate it's alleged ghosts, so in that respect too, it really was an honour. It was quite an event by all accounts with some of Carlisle's biggest names being in attendance, including the Lord Mayor of Carlisle, along with all the local media too.

So there you have it. A first-hand account of some of the ghostly goings-on from this magnificent bastion, and from one of the most accurate psychic mediums I have ever worked with.

The Great Keep of Carlisle Castle.

Mystery Mist in Botcherby

The area known as Botcherby was once a small village that was founded in 1170, but is now a large suburb of Carlisle. Originally, Botcherby was named 'Bochardby', after King William II (King Rufus) gave the land to one of his officers of the same name. It was not until the sixteenth century that the name was changed from Bochardby to Botcherby, which it has remained ever since. Back in February and March 2010, the local newspaper, the *News and Star*, printed a number of articles regarding an alleged ghost caught on film at a local off-licence shop on Durranhill Road. The articles, entitled 'Medium called in to contact Carlisle's Botcherby shop ghost' and 'Carlisle off-licence's unwanted Spirit scares off store staff', caused so much debate amongst the people of Carlisle it would be rather foolish to leave it out of this volume.

Two members of staff from the Simply Food & Drinks shop were astonished to see on their closed circuit television screens, a strange and most peculiar mist materialise from out of nowhere, drift around the screen for a while, before drifting in and out of the store on no less than ten occasions. The anomalous mist, it was said, could only be seen on the CCTV screen, with nothing odd or untoward being reported outside the store where the actual cameras were pointing. This is interesting, as many ghosts, in fact most ghosts, are either seen with the naked eye and not picked up on film, or they are caught on camera but not actually seen by the photographer at the time the picture was taken. It is a very rare occasion when one sees a ghost, and then also manages to photograph it.

The two shop assistants, Trish Nolan and Sonya Hird, are both adamant that what they saw on the screen that night was indeed a genuine apparition. Trish was reported to have been a total sceptic prior to seeing this 'vision', but was soon convinced of the existence of an afterlife. In fact, she wished she had *not* seen anything and would have preferred it if it had never happened. I must admit that watching the video footage of the mist as it moves around makes for interesting viewing. In some respects, it does resemble a figure in motion, especially the section of the footage where it moves onto the road and disappears from sight. However, playing devil's advocate here, I must also say that some sections of the film could resemble the blurred image of an insect or spider as it moves around in front of the screen. It is so hard to say for sure one way or the other, so I shall not.

A Simply Food & Drinks store like the one in Botcherby where spooky apparitions were recorded on CCTV.

The footage, which has become rather well-known and much viewed around the Carlisle area, has now spread, resulting in the film being shown around the planet. I know just how quick this can happen, especially when it comes to footage or photographs of the paranormal. Since the footage was posted on the newspaper website it has been downloaded more than 20,000 times, making the news in such far away places as China, Japan and the US. With this, there have been lots of 'explanations' brought forward to explain what was seen. Some theories, from both sceptics and believers alike, hold water, but some explanations are ludicrous to say the least. One person suggested that the ghost had been 'disturbed' by a number of workmen as they were renovating an alleged haunted house that stood across the road from the shop. In my experience, when haunted buildings are renovated, the ghosts in question usually show their annoyance by creating more disturbances in the actual building itself, rather than decide to go for a walk to the local store. Others have suggested that it is indeed a spider or an insect, or perhaps something else that could have obscured the cameras lens and so give the impression of a ghostly figure; such as car headlamps reflecting as they drive by. All potential answers to this baffling occurrence, but nothing that can be proven.

A couple of interesting aspects of this case came up when the shop manager, Sue McKie, decided to call in a medium to try and help get to the bottom of the mystery. Sadly, attempting to trace this medium and find out just what they thought yielded no results for me. Perhaps if that medium is reading this, they might like to come forward and tell me about their findings?

Of course, if a place is haunted then more often than not you get 'other' phenomena reported too; such as the displacements of objects, or perhaps localised cold spots. This did happen at the shop, with Trish Nolan reporting that she went ice cold prior to the mist making another appearance. Furthermore, Sue McKie pointed out that the store had six CCTV cameras installed, which had recently been randomly switching themselves on and off without human intervention. On top of that, the CCTV camera that was placed outside of the shop allegedly showed a light being turned on inside the shop during the night when no one was there. Sue decided to clean the lens of the camera to see if these anomalous images did indeed have a natural explanation, such as insects. Despite these efforts, the image was reported to have been seen again on just under fifteen occasions the following Saturday, and a further seven times on the Sunday. If the lens was cleaned – and I have no doubt that it was – then the insect theory, as much as it pains the sceptics, must be dismissed from the equation, leaving the mystery of the Botcherby mist open for more debate.

And more debate it created, with one fascinating response from a member of the public suggesting it could have been the ghost of a well-known money-miser who died back in the late seventeenth century. It is said that her house (or at least one of them) was on this very spot and the area in question was reputed to be haunted by this woman, who was known as Margery Jackson. It is said that after her death her ghost was seen in this area and was thought to be looking for the money that she had left behind after she had died.

Margery's ghost is also reputed to haunt a number of the council properties in and around this area, resulting in many applications for re-housing from the startled tenants. If these stories have any truth in them, and Margery Jackson's ghost does reside in this area of Carlisle, then maybe, just maybe, the anomalous mist that was recorded outside the Simply Food & Drinks shop could well have been her; we have more on Margery Jackson later on in this book and as you will shortly discover, I have found yet another house in which the old miser was said to have lived, and it is in the least likely of places!

Curses, Calamities and Catastrophes in Carlisle

In the early years of the new millennium, the BBC News ran an unusual story concerning a giant stone work of art that had been commissioned by the Carlisle Millennium Gallery, which had been placed on display between the gallery and Carlisle Castle, as part of the Millennium celebrations. Apparently, the artwork, which is known as the 'Cursing Stone', is thought to weigh up to a staggering fourteen tonnes, and is meticulously inscribed with a sixteenth-century hex, and is reported to have brought mayhem and disaster to Carlisle. Surely, this monument to the millennium could not have seriously caused the misfortunes that the city of Carlisle has endured since it was commissioned, could it?

Well, a good percentage of the Carlisle folk – fifty per cent in fact – seem to think it has. Since the stone was brought to Carlisle many bad things have occurred. This is something which cannot be denied, but is the stone really responsible? A local councillor, who believed the stone should be removed or even destroyed, stated that since the erection of the stone in the city, Carlisle had seen it all; fires, flooding, foot and mouth disease, job losses, even a lack of goals scored by Carlisle FC, and much more. The stone, which was the brainchild of acclaimed artist Gordon Young, is festooned with just 300 words of the original 1,069-word ancient curse, which was first cast by the Archbishop of Glasgow, Gavin Dunbar (c.1490-1547), in October 1525 to protect people from the border reivers who were feared, dreaded and most certainly hated throughout those ancient times. Interestingly, the artist himself, Gordon Young, descends from one such reiver family.

It is said that priests in the churches of every parish in what is now Cumbria, Northumberland, and Dumfries and Galloway were instructed to read it aloud to their respective congregations. It is also said that in George MacDonald Fraser's amazing work, *The Steel Bonnets* (1971), Archbishop Dunbar was 'among the great cursers of all time'. Plans to have the stone

The Cursing Stone. Some believe this artwork is at the centre of some of Carlisle's recent misfortunes.

removed from Carlisle were seriously considered after numerous Christian groups pre-warned the museum about its 'cursed' reputation. Petitions were signed in an effort to keep this harbinger of disaster away. After the spate of tragic events Carlisle had suffered, the motion was scheduled to have the stone removed. It was subsequently decided by the powers that be, that the stone would have simply cost the authorities way too much money to have it taken away. This, combined with the money that it took to make it and then have it brought in to the city, would have amounted to serious sums of wasted funds. Instead, the authorities decided to keep the stone, but have it blessed in a ceremonial ritual.

In one national UK newspaper the story began with, 'An "evil" sixteenth-century curse inscribed on a giant stone in Cumbria - the centrepiece of a £6.7 million millennium exhibition - is to be "exorcised" by an archbishop after clergy complained that it generated spiritual violence'. The Bishop of Carlisle, Revd Graham Dow, was in support of the local Christian groups and believed that a curse was in operation, which 'exerts a malevolent influence'. At the time, he recommended that the current Roman Catholic Archbishop of Glasgow visit Carlisle to bless the stone and lift the curse that had been invoked by his predecessor all those years ago.

This dismayed the local council, as, quite simply, they thought the work of art was exactly that and nothing more; a work of art. Even Gordon Young himself was upset at the prospect of being responsible for so much calamity in Carlisle, and was quoted as saying, 'had I known the stone would bring such bad luck to Carlisle FC I would have smashed the thing up myself'. I guess Gordon is a die-hard Carlisle FC fan. The council even arranged a meeting with the Revd Dow to discuss these concerns with him, showing that although they may not share his views, they respected them. The fact of the matter is, however, not all the people of Carlisle think the stone is cursed. Floods happen all over the world, people do lose their jobs, football teams more often than not suffer from goal droughts. My point is, all these disasters could well have happened even if the Cursing Stone had never been brought to Carlisle. This is something we must

not forget. Although keeping an open mind in regards to the paranormal, we must keep our feet on the ground and think rationally; it is no good jumping to paranormal conclusions, even if it does make a great Halloween tale.

Having said that, this debate goes on and on, and I have seen websites dedicated to it, advising people to keep well away – do not touch it; do not go anywhere near it for it will surely bring you bad luck, or worse. People do indeed have strong beliefs regarding occult matters, so it would be also most foolish and ignorant to suggest that they are wrong. Perhaps the stone *is* cursed by an ancient hex that was invoked over 500 years ago? Who knows? To end this section I was going to re-publish the entire curse – word for word – just so the reader could see what was said all those years ago, but I decided it would be in my best interests not to. After all, if the curse is true, then perhaps no one would have bought this book and it would be destiny for it to fail. We can't have that! Should you wish to see the full transcribed curse in all its glory, I suggest you pay the world wide web a visit. It's on a number of websites so if anything does go wrong for you after reading it, then at least we can all agree that I cannot be held accountable!

The Currock Road Spectre

During my research for this book I came across an abundance of fresh and new first-hand tales of ghosts from some of the good people of Carlisle. David Harkins, aged 52 and from the Upperby area of Carlisle, told me not one but two fascinating ghost tales connected to Carlisle. Here, in his own words, are David's accounts of his encounters with the paranormal:

Two occasions stand out for me. The first time was when I was still at school. I would have been about fourteen years old at the time, and I worked on the morning milk round for an old guy named Eddie Feddon, who was from Scotby; I think he has now sadly passed on. Anyway, we milk lads had to meet up with Eddie and his milk float at 4.45 in the morning, outside John Gardhouse's bakery shop, which is on Currock Road. From Gardhouse's shop we would deliver milk to houses all over Currock and Upperby and Harraby, and then go home, wolf down some breakfast before going to school where, speaking for myself, I would catch up on some sleep. Anyway, this particular morning I was late out of bed and therefore had to catch Eddie's milk float somewhere in the Currock Park Avenue area. As I was walking along Blackwell Road, passing Arnside House, just before you turn into Currock Park Avenue, I saw this little old woman wearing dark clothes and moving quickly backwards and forwards across Currock Road. She was crossing where the Methodist church is, and then re-crossing over again. From the opposite side of Currock Road, she would look over at the Methodist church. I stood and watched her do this about five or six times at least. I thought it was rather odd, but nevertheless carried on with my walk to meet the milk float. I later mentioned this to a friend's mother

who, surprisingly, then told me quite a few people had already seen this strange woman repeatedly crossing the Currock Road outside the Methodist church early in the morning. Even more surprisingly, my friend's mother explained that she knew who this woman was and that she had died suddenly a few weeks previously! The Methodist church was where her funeral had been only weeks before. Her spirit was confused, I guess.

This is an interesting story which deserves to be followed up and investigated thoroughly. For example, I would like to know who the other people were that saw the lady crossing the road, and what they thought of the incident. Also, David's friend's mother said she 'knew the woman' so an identity for the ghost lady could be revealed. Records will also show how she died and if she has any existing family. All these clues could yield more fascinating information that could provide, perhaps, an answer as to why she haunt's that area of Currock Road. This is something that I may pursue in the future; it certainly would be interesting to get to the bottom of it.

The Ghost of Mrs Kirkwood

David's second story is just as fascinating as the first and is centred not far from the main entrance to Carlisle's railway station, in an area known as the Crescent. He had been on holiday to Paris and had returned to Carlisle with his heavy luggage. As it was late and he was getting rather tired he did not want to suffer the rigmarole of catching the last bus, which would have seen him arrive home a lot later, so he decided to catch a taxi back instead. After standing for a few minutes, a taxi came around the corner. David continues the story:

An artist's representation of the ghost of the old lady that Carlisle resident David Harkins saw the night he came home from his holidays. (Courtesy of Julie Olley.)

As the taxi was coming round the crescent I saw a lady who just happened to live a few doors up from where I live on Scalegate Road, she was called Mrs Kirkwood – and she was waiting at the bus stop for the last bus. She used to go regularly to play bingo, and nearly always caught this last bus home. Anyway, I still do not know why to this day I didn't ask the taxi driver to stop so I could ask old Mrs Kirkwood if she wanted a lift home… but I didn't. She was such a distinctive lady and you couldn't really mistake her for anyone else. She always wore a headscarf and a long coat with a belt around, and she had her handbag of course; I can say it *was* indeed her. Anyway, I didn't ask the taxi driver to stop his car until I got back home and it was while I was unpacking my suitcase that I happened to mention to my mother that I had seen Mrs Kirkwood waiting at the Crescent for the last bus, and that I felt guilty for not asking the taxi driver to stop so I could have asked her if she wanted a lift home. My mother's reply was 'You'd have a queer job. She died two days ago'.

I have heard many stories just like this one and they never cease to amaze me. So many people experience a ghost in this way, the strange thing being that they don't even know they have actually seen a ghost until sometime after the event. I wonder what would have happened if David had indeed stopped the taxi and offered Mrs Kirkwood a lift home. Would she have disappeared into thin air, or would she have accepted the lift, giving David the opportunity to take a taxi ride – possibly engaging in conversation – with a ghost? That is an amazing thought! But alas, we will never know. My thanks go to David for allowing me to publish these fantastic accounts.

The Crown and Mitre Hotel

The Crown and Mitre Hotel is located in the centre of Carlisle, on English Street. It is, as their website states, 'the perfect mix of Edwardian grandeur and offers beautiful original features including a real log fire, an elegant sweeping staircase combined with all the modern comforts of home'. This, they say, gives the hotel a relaxed and welcoming atmosphere.

The Crown and Mitre Hotel was designed by George Dale Oliver and restructured by a building company named Beaty Brothers in the early 1900s, and was officially opened on 6 June 1905. In its earlier days, it was known as the Coffee House, which was some sort of music hall in which the renowned musician Paganini once played in 1833. The building, which dates back to the early 1700s, has been privy to much history and has seen many people come and go over the years. I have even discovered that it has also suffered its fair share of bloodshed. In 1746, it is said that a prisoner – along with other rebels – was 'quartered at his masters Ye Crown and Mitre', although I can't find out why. On 9 November 1927, a fire at the Crown and Mitre caused almost £5,000 worth of damage. The fire broke out in the stockroom but was quickly contained; just as well, as the whole building could have been lost forever, which would have been devastating. It was later renovated and transformed into the hotel, which is the one we see today.

Like most historical edifices, the Crown and Mitre is alleged to house a number of ghosts within its walls. I wanted to find out something, anything, about the alleged ghosts that are said to inhabit this wonderful old hotel, so I rang them up and spoke to the reception manager, Maggie McClellan. She told me that she had been in employment at the hotel for the last twelve years and when I asked her if the hotel was, as reputed, haunted, she replied with gusto, 'Oh yes, indeed it is'. She told me that she had heard hundreds of eerie tales from visitors and members of staff alike, all claiming to have had odd experiences at the hotel. I asked just how many ghosts are said to haunt the building and she informed me that there were three or four in total. She even told me of her own encounter with what she described as a 'strange presence' down in the lower level of the building. Although, she had not actually seen anything with her own eyes, she did say that on a number of occasions, she has felt as though she was being watched in this area. A sense of unease always envelopes her here, and like a lot of the other members of staff, she does not like being down in this area alone. I then asked Maggie to detail the ghosts that are said to haunt the hotel.

The first ghost, Maggie said, is thought to be that of a former night porter that once worked at the hotel. The ghost, who is called George, has not been seen since 2001. He is said to be wearing what is thought to be night porter attire – trousers and a jacket – and was observed in the basement area of the premises that is known as the supper room. This is the same area where Maggie admits to feeling uneasy whenever she is down there. I was informed that many members of staff

The Crown and Mitre Hotel, rumoured to be haunted by a number of ghosts.

The beautiful foyer of the Crown and Mitre Hotel.

still flatly refuse to venture down into the cellar area on their own, for fear of running into the ghost of George. I was informed that George had been a real person and had worked at the Crown and Mitre for many years prior to his death. George was believed to be a lovely fellow, friendly and courteous in life, however, his ghost seems to petrify the staff. It is interesting to note that in the 1891 census, the proprietor of the building is named as one George Pashley from Doncaster, who at that time was forty-nine years old. George also appears in the 1901 census, but by this point he had sold the premises. One wonders if this night porter ghost could in actual fact be the former building owner.

In more recent years, the shade of a young boy dressed in Victorian garb has also been seen down in the supper room. Again, this ghost is said to frequent the basement and has been seen by staff as he peers around a corner. No one knows who he is, or indeed why he haunts the hotel. As to why he is seen peering around the corner is anybody's guess; perhaps he is hiding from someone that had done him some harm in life? The last sighting of this spectre was by a member of staff who wishes to remain anonymous; this sighting occurred in 2010.

There are ghosts in the Ballroom too. Many people have reported seeing various figures flitting around the place when no one is supposed to be in there. Dark shadows move around, and phantom footfalls have been heard clumping across the floor by members of staff, once again whilst there is no

The basement area of the hotel, where the ghost of George was last seen in 2001. He is said to have been sighted wearing night porter attire, and was observed in the area known as the supper room.

The Ballroom – an area where many people have reported seeing various figures when no one was supposed to be in there.

one there. A smartly dressed man has also been seen leaning against one of the pillars in this area. At the time, nothing is thought of this sighting, that is until he slowly disappears into the pillar! Again, this spectre is an unknown ghost.

Maggie then went on to tell me that one of the hotel's management team spent the night in room 203, and was horrified to wake up in the night, at around 2 a.m., to see the distinct figure of a young boy standing at the foot of his bed. The phantom boy was leaning over the bed with both hands firmly pressed down upon the bottom of it, near to the witness's feet – and he was staring intently at him. The terrified member of staff jumped out of bed and vacated the hotel room; he has never used that room again!

I found the ghost tales of the Crown and Mitre so alluring I decided that I had to visit the hotel for a guided tour and a good look around. In the summer of 2011, I made a trip across to Carlisle to see Maggie, but sadly she was away on holiday's, so I missed her. I spoke to another member of staff and, explaining who I was, told them all about the arrangement I had with Maggie regarding a tour of the hotel. I was promptly shown around all the alleged haunted areas of the hotel by Maggie's brother, who was an extreme sceptic, and for this I am very grateful indeed. After my all-access tour of the hotel I was given the opportunity to explore the place freely and take the photographs that I needed for this volume; that done, I then said my goodbyes and moved on to my next haunted location.

The corridor of room 203, where a member of staff saw the ghost of a young boy standing at the foot of his bed.

The Ghost of Long Lane – Mary, Queen of Scots?

You may not think it, but Mary, Queen of Scots has quite a significant link to the city of Carlisle because this is where she was first imprisoned in England. Before we look at her connections to the city, let us first take a brief look at the woman herself. Mary Stuart, famously known as Mary, Queen of Scots, reigned as Queen of Scotland from 1542 to 1567 when she was forced to abdicate in favour of her son. She was the daughter of King James V of Scotland and Marie de Guise. She was born at Linlithgow Palace in Scotland on 8 December 1542, and was baptised at the church of St Michael, close to Linlithgow Palace. At the age of five Mary was sent to France to live after the King of France (Henry II) had pre-arranged the young queen's marriage to his then three-year-old son, François, who was the heir to the French throne. This pre-arranged marriage would ultimately unite France and Scotland. She stayed at St Germain, near Paris, for the next thirteen years. While in France, the young Mary received the best education and by the time she had finished her studies she was proficient in a number of languages including Italian, Greek, Latin, Spanish and, of course, French. In 1558, the pre-arranged marriage to the Dauphin François was carried out at *Cathedrale Notre Dame de Paris*. In 1559, after King Henry II died, Dauphin François became King of France and Mary then became Queen Consort of France, but because she had already been an anointed Queen of Scotland she did not take part in the coronation. In 1560, Mary's husband died and one year later she returned to Scotland.

In 1565, at Holyrood Palace in Edinburgh, Mary married Lord Darnley, but this marriage was doomed from the outset. Darnley became very pompous and arrogant and formed a hatred for the Queen's private secretary, David Rizzio. This hatred resulted in the brutal murder of Rizzio in front of the horrified queen inside Holyrood Palace in 1566. The room where Rizzio was murdered is now known as the Mary, Queen of Scots room, and it is reputed to be haunted. An irremovable bloodstain, from the unfortunate murder victim (who was stabbed repeatedly to death), is said to forever tarnish the floor of this room, returning time and time again despite efforts made to wash it away. I have been fortunate enough to have visited this room in Holyrood Palace and to have interviewed the palace guide. She told me that she had not had any paranormal experiences there of her own; she did say, however, that some of the other guides get certain feelings and impressions from this room. She went on to say that these guides do not like being in the Mary, Queen of Scots room alone and would prefer it if they did not have to use the room at all. I then asked if Queen Mary herself had ever been seen in here and was told that, as far as she knew, she had not.

In 1566, Mary gave birth to her son, James. In 1567, Mary was travelling back from Sterling to Edinburgh when she was kidnapped and taken to Dunbar Castle. It was not long after this when Mary, Queen of Scots became an enemy of the state, after marrying her third husband, the Earl of Bothwell. She had presumed that her nobles had consented to the marriage, but they had not. This resulted in the Scottish nobility turning against the newlyweds, to the point where they even raised an army against them. Mary was eventually captured and imprisoned at Loch Leven Castle near Kinross. In 1568, Mary escaped her captors and fled to England, landing in Workington in May 1568. She then went into protective custody – being looked after by Queen Elizabeth's soldiers – at Carlisle Castle. As far I can tell, this is the only link with Carlisle that Mary, Queen of Scots had; two months (18 May to 13 July) of protective custody. From there she was moved to Bolton Castle, in Yorkshire, before being moved to Tutbury Castle in Staffordshire. Mary's downfall began after eight handwritten letters (known as the Casket Letters) she had reputedly sent to the Earl of Bothwell, implicated her in the murder of her second husband, Lord Darnley. Nowadays, no one knows if these letters were authentic, but back in the day they were seen as proof of Mary's involvement in Darnley's death. Although the trial reached a verdict of 'not proven' (by order or Elizabeth I), Mary stayed in her protective custody until her later letters then further implicated her as sanctioning the Babington Plot. Essentially, the Babington Plot was an attempt, or at least a conspiracy to murder Queen Elizabeth I. Had the plot succeeded, Mary could have stepped into the breach, and become the Queen of England. Treason, then, was her crime and a sentence of death was duly passed.

At Fotheringhay Castle on 8 February 1587, Mary was beheaded. It is thought that it took the executioner two attempts to remove Mary's head, after the first blow made contact with the back of her head, and not her actual neck! 'Sweet Jesus' is what Mary is reported to have uttered as the axe was carelessly buried into her skull. So, that was the end of Mary, Queen of Scots. Or was it? It appears not, as her restless spirit is said to have come back from the dead, wandering the earth, forever in turmoil, visiting an abundance of places along the way. The ghost of Mary, Queen of Scots is said to haunt many locations, Bolton Castle being one of them, although when I visited, the owner's son, Lord Tom Orde-Powlett, told me that he didn't actually believe it himself. He said that the ghost that has been seen on a number of occasions could have been mistaken for her, although the rumours persist it is Mary. Tutbury Castle, in Staffordshire, lays claim to her phantom, as it allegedly meanders across the castle grounds and over the grass. Many people claim to have seen this ghost and have identified it as the former Queen of Scotland. In fact, it would be easier to list the places where the ghost of Mary, Queen of Scots has *not* been seen, because so many places she visited whilst alive now lay claim to having her ghost; and she is said to have visited hundreds of castles and stately homes. Her royal residences at both ends of Edinburgh's Royal Mile – Holyrood Palace and Edinburgh Castle – surprisingly do not claim to have her ghost, even though you would think these are the most likely places for her to haunt, after having

Above and left *Long Lane, where Queen Mary's ghost has reputedly been seen.*

at the castle. Syd very kindly informed me that, 'whilst at Carlisle, Mary, though a virtual prisoner, was still a "royal" and a "guest" of Elizabeth. With escort she was allowed to walk to the Cathedral, to go onto Castle Green to see her servants and the castle guards play "football" and perhaps to exercise or ride a little. She was at this point of her time in England not confined strictly within the castle walls'.

The interesting thing about this is that Long Lane is more or less en-route to Carlisle Cathedral, so it is very plausible that the imprisoned Queen of Scotland may well have taken this route to visit the cathedral. Having said that, just because she has been in that area does not necessarily mean she must haunt it, we need a little more information than that; and a little more information I attempted to get.

Sadly, this was where my research hit a brick wall. I telephoned an individual one day in the hope that this person could help me with my research. This someone, who shall remain nameless, knew a little more about this alleged ghost sighting than I did and I hoped that they might share with me the story for this publication.

spent so much time there. Stirling Castle, another place where she spent a lot of time, has a ghost of a Pink Lady; this, of course, is also thought to be that of Mary herself. Carlisle Castle does not lay claim to a Mary ghost, although, as stated earlier, she was held there for two months.

One of the sightings that has been reported in Carlisle, however, was said to be down in Long Lane, not far from where the castle stands. I contacted the Marie Stuart Society and asked the society's Honorary Secretary, Syd Whitehead, if it would have been at all possible for Queen Mary to have been allowed out to visit places whilst she was being held captive

Alas, this was not to be the case, and unfortunately I was unable to gather any more information on this story.

Nevertheless, I would still like to find out the full story behind the alleged ghost sighting of Mary, Queen of Scots in Long Lane, so if anyone out there can shed some light on it, or perhaps it was you who saw the ghost, please get in touch and do let me know.

Carlisle Cathedral, where the imprisoned Mary, Queen of Scots would come and worship during her captivity at Carlisle Castle.

Carlisle (Citadel) Railway Station

It's amazing the things you learn, isn't it? I have travelled through Carlisle and its railway station hundreds of times over the years; back and forth across the country in search of ghosts, visiting haunted sites in Scotland and in the Lake District, and all those times I was there – pacing the platforms as I made my way to my respective trains, or sitting on a train while passing through Carlisle and waiting for the train to pull out – I never realised I was so close to a number of ghosts already; in fact you could say I was sitting right on top of them, for underneath the railway station itself lies what is known as the 'undercroft' – a labyrinth of tunnels and passageways that has not been used by the railway authorities for well over thirty years, but dates back, however, over a century and a half. This almost long forgotten underground warren of stone tunnels and chambers is said to have been built on former slum dwellings which were known as the Fever Nests.

The station was built in 1847, at a cost of £53,000 and was jointly funded by the Lancaster and Carlisle and the Caledonian Railways primarily to serve the Cumbrian city that is Carlisle – although there were one or two stations already in Carlisle at that point. This now Grade II listed building, which was designed by notable architect William Tite, and subsequently built by the Brassy and Stephenson contractors, is now one of the major stations located on the west coast mainline. It has eight platforms and sees in excess of one million people pass through it every year. Out of those one million people, I wonder how many actually realise they are walking on top of a reputedly haunted location; I know I didn't.

Carlisle railway station has long had a reputation for being haunted, and not just by one ghost. There are, if the stories are to be believed, a whole plethora of ghosts residing there, all waiting for the unwary traveller to stumble across them. The undercroft areas, along with certain station rooms are 'notoriously haunted' according to the station staff, with strange sightings and even stranger sounds being reported on a regular basis. This area of the railway station was once said to have been used as a storage area, where it is believed they once kept animals; namely horses with their carts, and, on one occasion, elephants.

Many of the incidences of ghostly activity have been documented and recorded at the station, including the phantom of a young boy and a dog (there is a photograph in existence that was taken by the station manager, Stuart Davison, of the young lad and the dog). A man aged around fifty has been seen standing in one of the waiting rooms;

Carlisle railway station – home to numerous ghosts, including a veiled lady and a headless man.

An area of the undercroft at Carlisle railway station. This tunnel runs directly underneath a railway line and has been the scene of some terrifying paranormal activity.

a strange red mist has reportedly been filmed; and a ghostly figure has been photographed standing outside the station at three o'clock in the morning in the midst of a terrible blizzard. More harrowing encounters include the spine-chilling apparition of a veiled lady that paces around in the upper corridors, and the ghost of a headless man has been seen on platform 8.

These two spectres are believed to be related to one another, as we shall soon hear. The story behind the headless man haunting is quite gruesome and terribly sad. I discovered the origin of this tale after the station sub-manager, Sue Howarth, returned my telephone call asking for information about their alleged ghosts, in May 2011. By all accounts, a young couple that were deeply in love had eloped to Gretna Green to become husband and wife. As the train they were on was nearing Carlisle station, the young man decided to pull down the window of the carriage and stick his head out. Perhaps he was about to shout out the window in happiness to tell the world he had just gotten married, who knows?

Regardless, as he put his head out of the window it was subsequently decapitated by a thin piece of razor-sharp steel wire that was hanging down from one of the upper gantries. His head fell onto the rail tracks and his lifeless body collapsed in and slumped to the floor of the carriage – much to the horror of his new bride. When the train pulled into the station, it is said that the platform attendant opened the carriage door to find the distraught woman – still wearing her veil – cradling the headless and still twitching body of her beloved husband. From then on, it was said that the ghost of the headless young man haunted the area around platform 8, with his ghost being seen mostly in an area known as the 'four foot'. The four foot is the gravelled gap inbetween the two sets of lines that occupy this platform; this, of course, is the platform which the newlyweds train was pulling into. In fact, I later found out from Sue that two of her staff members at the station have actually reported seeing this headless ghost on the lines in the last few years. Sadly, they declined an interview.

The ghost of the aforementioned 'veiled lady' that has been seen wandering around in the upper section of the office areas is presumed to be the newlywed lady. She was, by all accounts, taken into the area where they now carry out the office duties and was cared for by the staff there.

The staff at the station have experienced so many ghostly goings-on, that they decided to open up the underground vaults and station for tours. 'Ghost Hunters get chance to spend night under Carlisle Rail Station' read the headline in the *News and Star*. At this point, the cynics may think, 'Ah-ha, just another money-making scheme invented to line their own pockets'. Not in this case. All monies raised on the ghost tours are donated to a local children's cancer research charity called CLIC Sargent.

A series of newspaper articles detailing the tours was published in the *Cumberland News* and thus the events were a massive success. Over twenty guided tours were

The corridor in the upper level of the main station building, where a ghostly veiled lady has been seen.

Platform 8, where the ghost of a headless man has been seen making his way along the middle of the tracks in an area known as the 'four foot'.

carried out, taking well over 400 people round the station and down below into the undercroft to experience, or at least hope to experience, the ghosts there. Considering that the sounds of a woman crying, hideous wailing, and other such ghastly noises have been reported there – as well as poltergeist-like activity being observed, such as doors slamming closed and then opening again on their own – the tours were more or less guaranteed to be nerve-racking to say the least.

At this point, let me make an observation. Take a huge group of over-expectant, paying, amateur ghost hunters and thrill seekers down into an area where they are told 'paranormal events' take place on a regular basis, and you would expect a large percentage of them to report ghostly goings-on – or events that could be described as paranormal in nature – when in actual fact, the likelihood is that they probably have perfectly normal origins. Many photographs of faces, shapes, lights etc. suddenly develop supernatural aspects, along with the usual physical phenomena; feelings of being touched, pulled, breathed upon etc.

You have to look at psychology here; most of the people attending these tours (and many other tours like them) are very likely primed before they even start, having been told what to expect and who haunts the area, or perhaps already knowing the ghost stories prior to the event; this automatically heightens the atmosphere, which includes, and most certainly induces, fear, especially for those who are die-hard believers. They then, without even realising it, seek out the paranormal explanation as opposed to a rational one whenever something remotely odd occurs. I have seen this occur hundreds of times on many investigations that I have been asked to attend.

Don't get me wrong, I love a good ghost story as much as the next person, but I also like to investigate hauntings in the best way that I can, by attempting to discover the truth behind them. I am not saying the undercroft is not haunted, on the contrary; there is much reliable evidence to suggest strange things do occur there which cannot be explained in a rational way. Indeed, I have spent the night there myself on a number of occasions during a series of privately and professionally run investigations, and have personally accumulated some fascinating data to support the stories. However, it must be stressed that not *all* of those on the ghost tours claiming to have experienced a paranormal incident actually did!

Let us not forget what these particular tours are about; raising money for a children's cancer charity. It does not matter whether what the public experienced was real or not, simply because each and every one of those attending are helping to raise funds for a good cause. For the record though, the station would not be doing these tours at all had it not been for the station staff reporting paranormal activity there for years. Activity that has

been experienced by people who were simply getting on with their everyday jobs, when ghosts were the last things on their minds; people who just turned up for work and got a little bit more than they bargained for; people that were not ghost hunting and were not primed with expectations; it is these ghost accounts that I am interested in.

During my telephone call with station sub-manager Sue, I had hoped to gain some more information regarding the ghosts of the train station. I got more than I hoped for when I was invited to Carlisle for a private tour of the train station and its undercroft, with a full lowdown of all the ghosts and the accounts that accompany them. So, on 29 June 2011, fellow ghost-hunter Mark Winter and I made our way to Carlisle for an exclusive ghost tour we would not forget. We arrived at the train station at around 12.30 p.m. and were met by station employee Tom Gorst. Tom promptly took Mark and I upstairs and into the offices, where we met Sue Howarth for the first time. After a ten-minute chat, both Mark and I were treated to a two-hour long tour of the entire premises. There are simply too many accounts of paranormal happenings to include in this chapter so I have whittled it down to the paranormal incidents that were witnessed by Sue herself.

Sue's office is on the second floor of the train station, as seen from the front of the premises. It is directly underneath the third floor, where the ghost of the veiled lady is said to walk. As well as hearing footsteps and strange noises coming from the third floor area, when she knew for a fact there was no one up there, Sue has had a few eerie encounters, actually in her office. The first occurred on one hot summer's day when she was working with one of her co-workers. For no reason, the air on the far side of the room turned ice-cold; noticeably colder than the rest of the room. Although they looked for a possible explanation, they could find none. The area stayed ice-cold for two hours. The second occurrence to affect Sue came, again, while she was working at her desk. Oddly enough, she was discussing the undercroft with a station manager who wanted to write something interesting about Carlisle railway station in the *Virgin Trains* internal magazine, when, suddenly, she began to hear a static buzzing-like sound close to her head; almost right in her ear. She stopped for a moment, shook her head and rubbed her ear, trying to figure out what it was, when, out of nowhere, she felt what she described as an index finger being pushed hard into the side of her neck. Was it the work of one of the station's many ghosts? Or something else? Sue is convinced it was a ghost, and I am inclined to think that Sue may well be correct.

Let me finish this section by telling you about some of my very own odd occurrences, experienced during my investigations at the station. On the night of our first paranormal investigation we attained some exceedingly odd results, which we were more than happy with. During the guided tour of the station offices, at 8.45 p.m. on 6 August 2011, we experienced some odd readings in the electromagnetic field that were *not* registered during the baseline test that we had performed earlier. This event

occurred in the records room on the upper levels of the building. It seemed that we had discovered an anomaly within the natural electromagnetic field, as both the normal EMF meter and the K2 meter registered irregular readings; and interestingly, both meters seemed to respond to all of the questions we subsequently asked the alleged spirits. However, during our night vigils, that particular anomaly within the electromagnetic field was not registered again. So, prior to the investigation and during the investigation the irregularity was not detected, yet on the tour, during our attempts at communication, it was. An interesting aspect of scientific paranormal research that goes a little way to suggest something paranormal may have been going on.

A number of other incidences occurred during the course of the night, including the sighting of a ghost on a flight of stairs, inside the office area of the station. The apparition was seen for only a split second or so and it seemed to be following us up the stairs. Drew Bartley, a good friend and fellow investigative team member, was the last person through the doors at the top of the stairs, and was just closing the door when he was pushed out of the way by someone who was in quite a hurry, and he was almost knocked over due to the observer of the possible apparition wanting another look down the stairwell, after catching a glimpse of the figure through the glass window. However, since there was only one individual that claimed to have seen the ghost, and no other scientific proof exists to support this sighting, unfortunately it

The records room – peculiar spikes on the EMF meter and the K2 were recorded in this room, indicating that there could have been a spirit present.

has no evidential value whatsoever. There is one consolation for me, however; I know the apparition was indeed seen that night, because it was me who saw it.

The only other strange occurrence came in the early hours of the morning while a number of people were investigating an area known as the 'butcher's meat chamber'. Drew Bartley, Paul Dixon (of the Ghosts and Hauntings Overnight Surveillance Team), station manager Stuart Davison, and myself, were investigating the long pitch-black chamber when, suddenly, we all became aware of what can only be described as a sobbing woman. I looked at Drew, he looked at me and we both said together, 'What the hell was that?' The sound

seemed to come from close by, but inspection proved that no one – certainly no woman – was in this vicinity. Sadly, no recorded evidence of this event took place, even though two video cameras were rolling at the time. Paul's camera did not pick up the sound, unfortunately, but Drew's video camera was a different story. It appears that just at the point where the mysterious cry was heard, Drew's camera was somehow interfered with. When you view the tape, just at the crucial point the footage cuts to blank tape. The blank tape plays for a few seconds before cutting back to the undercroft footage, essentially cutting out the anomalous sobbing. We all heard this sound down in that chamber and it's a mystery as to why it was not

The stairwell, the site of a possible haunting.

The dark underground chamber where the distinct sound of a sobbing woman was heard.

recorded on tape. It is as though it was engineered on purpose by whoever, or whatever, resides down there. Whatever occurred, we know it was most certainly an odd thing to experience.

The Glasshouse Tunnel Ghost

Public houses are a facet of the ghost-hunting experience that no paranormal researcher can avoid. Wherever you go — with the exception of Antarctica, perhaps — you'll find a drinking den and, if you push hard enough, you'll find someone in that establishment who claims to have seen a ghost in there. But some haunted pub stories are different, for it's not so much the spectres *within* the pub that cause a stir, but those that manifest themselves *underneath*.

In Carlisle, there is a pub called the Friar's Tavern, a public house of quite ancient provenance. Or at least, it used to be called the Friar's Tavern. Over time it became simply FT's, and finally (at the time of writing) The Glasshouse. The name changes, but the old pub remains the same. As does what's underneath it, specifically a tunnel. Now, it has to be said that beneath the picturesque streets of Carlisle there are many tunnels. Some stand alone, others are linked. Some were built during the Victorian era, others at a much earlier date. The tunnel beneath The Glasshouse is said to be accessible through an arched doorway, which is now bricked up. But where does it lead, and what is – or was – its purpose? According to some, it is a Victorian sewer. This may be the case, but then again it was not unknown for Victorian architects and planners to utilise already existing facets of the environment when they were building. The tunnel may have been excavated in Victorian times, but it may have a much longer history. The tunnel is said to lead to the West Wall of the cathedral, which suggests that it may have been a bolt-hole for 'the religious' to escape through when they were being persecuted during the reign of Henry VIII. The sad truth is that we simply don't know. But the tunnel, whatever its origins, is said to be well and truly haunted.

Not surprisingly, given its age, location and state of repair, the tunnel rarely receives visitors. However, some who have gained entry and explored its darker recesses claim to have had some very strange experiences indeed. Details about the haunting are vague, and first seemed to gain common currency in the early 1960s, when reports came into circulation that a 'ghost' or 'entity' inhabited the tunnel. Curiously, it was said to travel between both entrances of the passageway, back and forth without ceasing. What was it? The ghost of a priest desperately attempting to find a safe haven as he was

The public house formerly known as Friar's Tavern, a site with haunted tunnels below it.

pursued by persecutors? Perhaps, but we can't be sure. In fact, how it is known that the phantom constantly travels back and forth along the tunnel is a mystery in itself. Other visitors have reported not visual anomalies, but auditory ones. Some have reported odd sounds that are both hard to identify and even more difficult to describe. Others have heard the sound of footsteps – those of the spirit, perhaps – that were most certainly not made by the investigators themselves.

And then there are the knockings; bizarre taps and thumps which, again, have no obvious origin. Whether these are connected to the same ghost that haunts the tunnel we simply cannot say, but it is a possibility.

Within the tunnel it is said that there are branches leading off in different directions, although at least some of them are now bricked up, and not all of them are immediately obvious. On occasion, the sounds have been heard emanating from behind the bricked-up recesses, almost as if someone, or something, was trapped in there. To get to the bottom of the mystery it would be necessary to excavate and explore the tunnel to see whether it truly stands alone or, as has been suggested, if it is connected to other passageways underneath Carlisle. A professional opinion would need to be solicited in regards to the origin of the tunnel; when it was built and for what purpose it served. Then, and only then, could we begin to hazard a guess at to the nature of the phantom said to reside there. Whatever the truth, there is an enigma beneath the pretty streets of Carlisle which definitely merits further investigation.

The Brickyard

The Brickyard is the name of a popular music venue located at 14 Fisher Street in central Carlisle. It is Carlisle's only full-time independent live music venue and was recently nominated for the *NME*'s Britain's best small venue award in 2011. Its website states that: 'The Brickyard is Carlisle's premier and only full time live music venue and has hosted some of the biggest names in music past and present. Formally known as The Richmond Hall, or The Richmond Memorial Hall, the venue itself is over one hundred years old and has been a key figure in the Carlisle music scene. The Richmond Hall was built as Saint Mary's Parish Rooms, named in honour of the late Canon Thomas Richmond of Carlisle Cathedral. After a long absence, the Richmond Hall was renovated and its doors opened on New Year's Eve 2002 to the new name of The Brickyard. Ideally situated between Newcastle and Glasgow, The Brickyard is a three hundred and twenty capacity venue'. Maybe room for a few more I think, if you include the dead patrons that are said to reside there in the form of its resident ghosts. I had read in the *Cumberland News* that the local ghost walkers stopped at The Brickyard during their tour, and that was all I needed to make contact fairly promptly, emailing the establishment with the following:

> Hello. My name is Darren and I am from Newcastle-upon-Tyne. I am writing a book on the ghosts of Carlisle (Haunted Carlisle) and I am looking for a little assistance. I once read an article in the Cumberland News about a ghost walk that every now and again occurs in Carlisle. In this article, it mentions that The Brickyard features on the tour, but that's all it says on the matter. I was wondering if indeed The Brickyard has a ghost and, more so, would you like the ghost story published in my forthcoming book. If the answer is yes to these questions then I

The Brickyard on Fisher Street. Formally known as the Richmond Memorial Hall, this building is over one hundred years old and has been subjected to strange happenings, leading people to suspect it may be haunted.

would be very grateful if you could fill me in about the history of the building, and its reputed ghosts (no matter how short the ghost tale may be). Do you have any literature that you could email me with the information on? Failing that, I will be visiting Carlisle on a number of occasions over the summer to research the book, so if it could be arranged, I could pop in during one of my visits.

Do let me know your thoughts on this matter, and I look forward to hearing from you soon.

Darren W. Ritson.

The following day The Brickyard emailed me back with the following:

Hi Darren, thanks for getting in touch. I don't know a great deal about the history of The Brickyard, sorry. I've only ever managed to find a couple of old newspaper articles from the record office at Carlisle castle, I have them down at The Brickyard which I can scan and send to you if you like? From what I can remember, it was originally a church which opened in 1906 and has been used as lots of other things since then; a pool hall, hairdresser, radio station and, more recently, a live music venue. My gran said she read something in the local paper sometime last year about a ghost at The Brickyard called Humphrey but she forgot to keep the paper. According to my gran, he was a roofer who fell and died. I've been working at The Brickyard for three years now and haven't heard or seen anything myself although when I'm there on my own, especially at night,

I do get the feeling I'm being watched; it's very eerie when all the lights are off. My colleague Andy has been there for ten years and hasn't mentioned seeing anything either. But...my friend who was up recording in The Brickyard (from Grimsby) one weekend, started pretty early, around 6 a.m. He was playing some music while lugging gear down the stairs and heard some whistling which he hadn't noticed in the song before. He said he played the song back but, strangely, he couldn't hear the whistling. Also our new sound engineer stopped back late one night recently and said he saw a dark figure move past the windows inside the venue. There hadn't been any talk or mention of ghosts so it was a little out of the blue when he brought it up. Those are the only two tales I have for you at the moment. If you wanted to speak to both of the guys who had those encounters I'd be happy to pass on their phone numbers/emails. Thanks a lot and please let me know if you do decide to include The Brickyard in your book or if you come across any other info on The Brickyard in your research.

Kind regards, Mark

I found Mark's reply very interesting to say the least. Particularly the strange occurrences regarding the incidences that happened to his colleagues who had spent time in the building. Of course, by now my whistle had been whet, and I simply had to follow these stories up. The contact numbers of the witnesses and the old newspaper scans seemed too good an opportunity to miss, so I decided to follow up this story. I emailed Mark back:

The old Memorial Hall sign.

Mark then replied to my email, which included the telephone numbers of the two individuals he had previously mentioned. Eager to find out just what had been witnessed I telephoned the first of the numbers, which belonged to Sam Kane. Sam was more than happy to talk to me about his encounter so I began my short interview, asking what he had experienced and when. Sam told me that it happened one night in January 2009. He had been in the building with two other colleagues and was preparing to do some recording. Realising he had forgotten to do something, he nipped out of the room to carry out his chore. He left his colleagues for only a few moments and it was then that he heard something really strange.

As he was making his way through the building he was startled to hear a loud whistling sound – or a screech – that sounded very much like feedback. 'The only thing was,' he said, 'none of the equipment that *would* have or *could* have produced a "feedback" sound, was plugged in'. I asked if his friends could have plugged something in without him knowing but I was told 'most certainly not because if they had plugged in an amplifier or something of that nature, they surely would have heard the whistling noise too … and they did not'. Sam told me that he tried all ways and means to work out just what the noise could have been or where on earth it could have come from. He explained to me that he was a sceptical individual and did not believe in 'ghosts' or 'paranormal activity', yet this incident had him perplexed. He still believes to this day that there must be a rational explanation for the strange sound, but what it could have been still eludes him to this day.

I was just about to wrap up the phone call with Sam when he mentioned something else, which was, in my eyes, even more eerie than the strange noise he had heard. Not long after he had heard the whistling sound, and while he was making his way back to his colleagues, he was stopped in his tracks by the enchanting sound of children singing. He told me that it sounded like a class full of youngsters all singing together. This, he admits, sent chills down his spine and he has no qualms with admitting he was quite scared. He searched the premises and even looked outside but could find no source at all for the sound. After listening to this 'children's choir' for a good three to four minutes it suddenly ceased. He then proceeded to tell me that he had heard the building was once a children's home/school. Make of that what you will.

Another account of strange occurrences in The Brickyard comes from James Heasley. His encounter occurred in June 2011, and, just like Sam's, it happened in the early hours of the morning at around 4 a.m.

He was spending the night at The Brickyard after doing some work and was having a few drinks with a friend. After leaving the room for a moment he walked past an area near to the kitchen. There was a door with a frosted glass panel and it was through this glass panel that he saw the shape of a man walking past behind the door.

This terrified James as he knew there was no one else in the building apart from his friend, who he had left back in the room they had been in. He swiftly opened the door and ran into the corridor to see who was there, half expecting to be confronted by a burglar, but was very surprised to find no one there. After searching the building inside out for traces of a break in, and finding none, he concluded that his encounter must have been a paranormal one. When James openly told me that he had been having a few drinks during the night he spent there, I asked him just how much 'drink' he had had, and he told me ' only a few cans' but assured me he was not drunk. Hardly enough to bring on hallucinations; come to think of it, alcohol is not an hallucinogenic at all so it does not matter how much he had had. That aside, I think we can safely say there are enough spooky tales and anecdotal accounts to suggest that there may indeed be something odd going on at The Brickyard music venue.

Laser Quest

Castles, public houses and old ruins are the stereotypical haunts of ghosts in the eye of the general public. Some may have even heard of factory units and even domestic dwellings that are said to play host to a ghost. But a playground called Laser Quest, surely not; yet, Laser Quest in Carlisle is said to be haunted.

So, for the uninitiated, just what is Laser Quest? The company's own website describes it as '... the world's best known and most exciting brand of Laser tag game [...] Each player is equipped with state of the art laser tag equipment and the game is played in a uniquely styled labyrinth which features custom built scenery, ramps, catwalks, lighting effects, swirling fog and futuristic music [...] Points are scored when you successfully zap your opponent on one of the many sensors located on the pack and gun. But beware, if you are zapped you lose points and get knocked out of the game for a few seconds'.

Great stuff, but not all the fun and games at Laser Quest are electronically-generated, it seems. Members of staff have reported strange occurrences in the building; so much so that some of them have begun to feel distinctly uncomfortable when they are locking up alone at night. On a visit there, back in October 2011, I was told this by manager, Dougie Kerr, 'It's not the entire building that is haunted, apparently, but only certain parts of it, including the entrance foyer at the foot of the stairs'. Dougie then told me that strange figures had been seen through the glass panels on the door that leads to the bottom of the stairs when no one should have been there, and when staff went over to investigate, they found themselves at the foot of the

Laser Quest; built on the site of the former prison, this venue is thought to be the home of a ghost that mysteriously appears and disappears during bouts of Laser Quest in the dark.

stairwell on their own. Some people have reported feeling very uncomfortable on the stairwell. Researchers sometimes refer to this as a 'sense of presence'. To be honest, it's hard to explain just what a 'sense of presence' is, except to say that it is an indefinable feeling that one is not alone, or that there is something disturbing and unsettling at that location. One may not be able to see anything or hear anything, but nevertheless it becomes impossible to shake off the feeling that someone, or something, is lurking nearby. Now it must be admitted that this 'sense of presence' or heightened awareness can often have a rational explanation. The ambience, electromagnetic fields, infrasound, the atmosphere and even the structure of a place can generate all sorts of emotions within visitors. Now, Laser Quest not only has such an ambience, but it is deliberately engineered to do so. Step inside, don your equipment and you can then enter a futuristic world, which is reminiscent of *Alien*, *Star Wars* and *Predator* simultaneously. To add to the eeriness, clouds of vapour are filtered throughout, hiding the combatants from each other. Could the staff at Laser Quest simply be imagining things, then? Could the eerie atmosphere simply be making the workers feel creepy, thus allowing their imaginations to take over and do the rest? It is possible, of course, but in this case I'd have to say unlikely.

Talking to Dougie Kerr during my visit, I got the impression that he was sincere and genuinely believed that there may be something paranormal occurring. Another member of staff I spoke to on my visit, Dave Maclachlan, told me he was very sceptical about ghosts and never believed a word anybody said about them; that was until he began to experience some strange activity for himself. He informed me that the lights often flash on and off when he is in the building alone, and he often hears strange, unexplained noises in areas where he knows no noises should be coming from. 'This does not occur anywhere else,' he told me, 'only when I am here in this building do these

things occur to me and this is why I am now open to the idea of something potentially otherworldly being here. My own experiences, combined with other people's accounts, in addition to the building's history, has really made me change my tune.'

But it's not just members of staff who have experienced the strange phenomena, some gamers have seen

The stairwell at Carlisle Laser Quest, where dark shadows and other unexplained figures have been seen through the glass window just out of shot to the right.

apparitions too. During combat sessions and periods of time in the game zone, it has been reported that a strange figure has appeared mid-game amidst the smoke and pandemonium, leaving those that see it bewildered and confused as to who it is. Within the blink of an eye the figure is gone, disappearing as mysteriously as it appeared. Sceptics might suggest that the figure is one of the team players, or gamers, and is simply mistaken in their judgement; however, the people who have seen this strange figure describe it as someone that 'doesn't seem to fit within the present environment', adding that 'the figure is not dressed in game attire'. Guess it's not a gamer then.

The Laser Quest haunting is well known, and has even garnered the attention of the press. A feature mentioned in the *News & Star* of 1 October 2009 reported on the spooky goings-on there. Reporter Pam McLounie explained that, 'Staff at Laser Quest – where Carlisle prison used to be – have heard noises and are scared to lock up when alone in certain parts of the building'.

So, given all the above, it is clear that it isn't just that creepy feeling or heightened sense of awareness that staff are experiencing, they are also hearing bizarre noises and seeing odd things. This is a little harder to explain away. Of course, just because one hears a noise or sees something out of the ordinary, which is difficult to explain, doesn't mean that it is something supernatural. There are a multitude of explanations – rational explanations – for bumps, thumps, bangs and strange sightings. In fact, in the majority of alleged hauntings, researchers

Dougie Kerr and Dave Maclachlan from Carlisle Laser Quest.

will inevitably find, after a little digging, that the anomalous phenomena reported has a perfectly rational explanation.

However, in the case of Laser Quest, workers and staff have reported seeing things and hearing noises that could, just possibly, have had an origin in the paranormal. So, if Laser Quest really is haunted, what could the explanation be?

Firstly, the building itself may be subjected to haunting. Something may have occurred on the premises at some time in the past – perhaps a sudden death, or even a murder – that has caused the haunting to exist. A detailed study of the building's history may shed more light on this. However, some hauntings are said to be attached not to the building itself, but to another which may have stood on the same site at a previous time. The haunting may well be a 'residue' from a previous era and just happens to be occurring on the land where the Laser Quest building now stands. Considering that the Laser Quest building is situated on the site of the old prison, where hangings used to take place, it could be that a lost soul, or a spirit or two, still lingers there. One local researcher has even suggested that Laser Quest actually stands on the site of the prison graveyard. The haunting may well be caused by the restless spirit of an old lag from days gone by, but what he makes of Laser Quest is anybody's guess.

The Ghost of Margery Jackson

Unfortunately, some ghost stories have a very short shelf-life. They appear briefly, like brightly shining lights, only to become extinguished by other stories and dramas which are deemed to be of greater importance. Others, however, survive over the generations and even now have the ability to captivate us. The following events relate one such tale.

Margery Jackson was known as the Miser of Carlisle – hardly a flattering title. She was baptised into 'the Body of Christ' at St Mary's Church, Carlisle, on 22 February 1722. Margery's father was a merchant whose business was centred in Carlisle itself. Her mother, Isabella, was the daughter of William Nicholson, who had strong Church connections; his cousin was a bishop. There was also a military thread running through the family. Her grandfather had been a

'Roundhead' in Oliver Cromwell's army during the English Civil War, and established a reputation as a dyed-in-the-wool soldier, his nickname being 'Trooper Tom'.

Little is known of Margery's early life; at least, little that can be proven. We do know that she worked in London as a maid for some time, but, when one of her brothers died, she returned to Carlisle, confident that she would inherit both property and money as a result. Alas, she was to be bitterly disappointed, as she was informed upon her arrival that the inheritance she had expected had actually been given to another relative. What made things worse was that the person who had inherited the property was only on the periphery of her extended family, and had not been as close to her brother as she had been. It was true that this closeness was merely a biological one, as the two had never got along when forced to endure each other's company, but Margery, both baffled and angry, decided to take her claim to court.

The case was to be heard in the Chancery at London. Margery, who was penniless, was forced to travel to the capital on foot. When the case was heard, she explained to the judge why she believed the inheritance was rightfully hers. She lost, her words falling on deaf ears. Her life from this point onwards was consumed with legal hearings – always regarding money, property and wills – but she stubbornly refused to accept the inevitable. Relatives and acquaintances regularly found themselves on the business end of solicitors' letters emanating from her counsel in London.

On occasion, her life took a favourable turn and she would find herself in possession of considerable wealth. On other occasions she would be destitute. And all the while, her bitterness became more acute and her desire for revenge stronger; it twisted her personality and, inevitably, she became eccentric. This is unfortunate, as she was once considered a pleasant young lady and contemporary records indicate that she was well clothed and well cared for. But all that was to change after the woman was robbed of her inheritance, some claims of which, as the evidence suggests, were entirely valid.

Margery started to dress in drab, old clothes and became a complete miser. She hoarded money, in all probability to help pay her burgeoning legal bills, which were considerable. She also hoarded money just for the sake of it. Her eccentricity gave her a penchant for gold coins. She hated bank notes, which, for some reason, she believed were 'of the Devil'. As her eccentricity developed, she declined to look after her home, the windows of which were filthy and the furniture caked with dust. And then, after a short illness, she died, and it was at this time that things took an interesting twist.

Years passed, and her home was demolished. A farmhouse was built on the site, and almost immediately the residents claimed that it was haunted. The shade of an elderly, unkempt woman was seen on numerous occasions, and few harboured any doubts that it was that of Margery Jackson.

But then the farmhouse was demolished, and houses were erected on the site. For a while, the spectre

One of the many homes of the 'Carlisle Miser', Margery Jackson. Surrounded by scaffolding, this old structure is now being incorporated into the main building, which you can see to the right of the picture.

of Margery Jackson seemed to rest – sightings were few and far between – but then, in 1962, a tenant saw her once again. The spirit form of Margery was back. Intriguingly, a local historian determined that the ghost wore clogs, as Margery always did, allegedly.

So, if Margery was haunting the place where her house had once stood, what could her motive have been? Well, we know that when she passed away a large chest containing thousands of pounds was discovered. Some said the contents were worth £10,000, others claimed it was nearer to £30,000. All were in agreement, however, that the contents were the gold coins she had treasured in real life. Was her spectre looking for the money she had secreted away? We may never know.

However, there is another possibility for Margery's appearance. She had made some bitter enemies during her life, including members of her own family. Till her dying day she was convinced they had robbed her of a sizeable inheritance. Had Margery Jackson, then, returned to hunt down those who had cheated her when she was alive? Did she, in spectral form, harbour ideas about appearing to her enemies and confronting them about her ill-treatment?

Tales of spectres coming back to haunt those who have wronged them are not uncommon, but, again, we may never know. Perhaps she had returned from the spirit world to right several wrongs?

The Ghost of Carlisle Cathedral

Carlisle is a place where layer upon layer of history has been laid down, each covering the last like a blanket. The people of Carlisle are renowned for their friendliness and optimism. They've had to be optimistic, for, over the centuries, their

city has been subjected to a great degree of turbulence, upheaval and bloodshed. Carlisle is just south of the Scottish border and has thus been occupied many times by sundry armies and factions. The Romans constructed a fort there, its purpose being to provide support for the legendary Roman Wall. Later, King William II built a castle there, as we know.

Because the landmarks in Carlisle's history were crucial stepping-stones in the eventual arrival of Christianity, which in turn led to the building of a cathedral, it is the cathedral at Carlisle where we now turn our attention. The city of Carlisle has had a very turbulent history. The Romans built a wall through it, Vikings invaded it and the Scots and English fought over it for many years. The cathedral was founded in the year 1122; over 1,000 years after Jesus walked the earth. Whether the teachings given in sermons there accurately represented the beliefs of the carpenter from Nazareth or not are another issue, but there is no doubt that this magnificent edifice made a great impact upon Carlisle's residents, and it still does.

The architecture of the cathedral is fascinating. Look at the pillars or columns and you will see beautiful, intricate medieval carvings representing many activities associated with human activity; all snapshots from a bygone era. As one gazes at the stained-glass windows and inhales the aroma of age, it is easy to think that the past is gone and all that we are left with are echoes. But this may not be true, for at least one remnant of the past is said to be 'alive' at the cathedral, and visible to privileged witnesses, in the

Carlisle Cathedral; said to be haunted by a phantom monk.

An artist's representation of the ghost monk of Carlisle Cathedral, reported to have been seen walking through a solid wall. (Courtesy of Drew Bartley)

form of a spectral monk. Stories about the ghost monk of Carlisle Cathedral are hard to authenticate, but they are nonetheless fascinating.

The first relates that a former Dean entered the cathedral and happened to see a monk walking down an aisle. Before he had the opportunity to even attempt to communicate with the man, the monk simply walked *through* a wall and disappeared. Later, a young girl attended service at the cathedral with her family. After a while, she started waving at someone, which baffled those in close proximity to her, as they couldn't see whom she was waving to. Later, whilst being questioned, she described the person in some detail and her description exactly matched that of the ghostly monk seen earlier by the Dean. Later still, Canon Phythian Adams testified to the existence of the ghost, although whether he actually saw the spectre himself is debatable.

Not all the ghosts are seen within the interior of the cathedral. A cavalier has been seen nearby, and in 1868 witnesses reported a 'midget' dressed in clothes fashionable from an earlier era, with silver buckles on his shoes. The 'midget', spotted in a nearby street, promptly vanished.

So, what are we to make of these stories? It is intriguing that the young girl who witnessed the spectral monk described him in exactly the same way as the Dean. To my knowledge there is no evidence to suggest that the child knew the Dean or, for that matter, that she had heard of the ghost stories connected to the cathedral. This has to be either an extraordinary coincidence or, more likely, evidence that both sightings may well have been genuine.

If the cathedral is haunted, the obvious question is, why? Could it be that its spiritual ambience and religious aura make it easier for ghosts to appear there? Or does the answer lie in its long and turbulent history? We may never know, but whatever the reason, there seems little doubt that this spectacular example of Christian architecture may not just cater for living worshippers, but also dead ones.

The Carlisle Cavalier

The English Civil War broke out in the early 1640s, and between 1644 and 1645 Carlisle and its castle was under siege. Royalist Carlisle was more than equipped, weapons wise, to withstand this attack. However, the Parliamentarians had another cunning plan up their sleeves. They decided to surround the castle, do absolutely nothing, and *starve* out the Royalists. Eventually, in late 1645, the Royalists could take no more of the misery and hunger they had suffered for nigh on nine months, and Carlisle was surrendered. Of course, wherever there has been civil war action there are always reports of civil war ghosts. Marston Moor in Yorkshire is a prime example of this, with an abundance of accounts, mostly reliable, to suggest that this particular area is indeed haunted. It's a shame that we cannot say the same for the next location.

The area around the West Walls of Carlisle, where the ghost of a cavalier from the English Civil War is said to haunt.

Throughout the paranormal community, rumour has it that down by the old West Walls, which once encircled this great city, resides the ghost of a civil war cavalier. Not much is known about this particular haunting, other than the fact that the area is reputed to be haunted by this soldier. In fact, you could say nothing at all is known about it. There is no forthcoming information regarding this spectre, and any reliable sightings date back to goodness knows when. This leads me to think that this account may indeed be a false one, unless of course someone comes forward with a recent sighting, or to shed some light on the earlier alleged sightings. Most ghost tales, when investigated, always seem to throw up something that leads the investigator down one path or another, but in this instance that is not the case. Someone, somewhere, must have details as to the early sightings of a ghost soldier in these parts. Until we get further information regarding this ghost, we must safely assume that this account is nothing more than a folk tale and not a genuine account of paranormal activity. Shame!

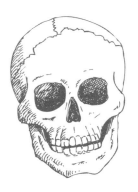

2

Ghosts on the Outskirts

The Wailing Ghost of John Whitfield

A few miles outside of Carlisle is Barrock Park and Barrock Hill, where, in 1777, the notorious highwayman John Whitfield was gibbeted alive for his heinous crimes of robbery and murder. It is said that he hung naked in his gibbet cage, suffering for a whole week. He was mentally and physically tortured by the elements, suffering from starvation and horrific muscle spasms due to his 'restricted moving space' in his gibbet cage, before a passer-by heard his pathetic moans of agony and shot him in the head out of mercy.

It was said that for many years after his painful death, the cries of anguish and his pitiful moans and groans could be heard by travelling men, reverberating in the area where his gibbet post once stood. Those who heard the harrowing screams and wails were convinced that it was the ghost of the infamous highwayman.

Whitfield's reign of terror came to an end after a failed attempt of robbery. After seeing a man out riding on his horse he decided to accost the fellow who, much to the dismay of Whitfield, fought back. Surprised by this, he drew his weapon and callously shot him point blank. Startled by the gunshot, the man's steed reared up before galloping off, carrying the almost dead man back to his home. There, he fell from his horse and died soon after from his wounds, without identifying his attacker.

Fortunately, a young scamp that happened to be in the area at that time, heard the commotion and watched in trepidation as the horror unfolded. During the struggle between the two men it is said that one of Whitfield's coat buttons was ripped off and fell to the ground. The youngster had the good sense to pick up the highwayman's button after the ruckus, and it was this crucial piece of evidence – along with his eyewitness testimony – that helped to put an end to John Whitfields' reign of terror.

Whitfield's reputation was a fierce and violent one. During his fearsome supremacy it is said that no one would

A gibbet post, similar to the one where highwayman John whitfield met his fate.

Stand and Deliver! An artist's illustration of the notorious highwayman John Whitfield. His ghost is still said to haunt the Barrock Park area of Carlisle. (Courtesy of Julie Olley)

near to where John Whitfield died. It is still thought by some that on quiet mornings, between midnight and sunrise, you can hear the tormented, yet distant cries of John Whitfield as they echo eerily around the area. It seems he is forever caught between two worlds, due to the odious crimes he once committed and for the punishment he so justly deserved.

The Radiant Boy, Corby Castle

Corby Castle, on the outskirts of Carlisle, is a privately owned family home that was originally built in the thirteenth century. The Salkeld family, who, incidentally, also owned the nearby hall bearing the family name, Salkeld Hall, constructed it out of red sandstone. The castle was sold in the early seventeenth century, to Lord William Howard, who was the third son of Thomas Howard, the 4th Duke of Norfolk. From this point on Corby Castle has always been known as the ancestral home of the Howard family. However, in the early 1980s Sir John Howard Lawson sold the property to Edward Haughey OBE, Baron of Ballyedmond, who then sold its contents and fully refurbished the castle. It is used nowadays as his family home and a venue for both business functions and private parties and entertainment. The ghost of Corby Castle, according to Jack Hallam in his book *Ghosts of the North* (1976), has not been seen for many, many years now; in fact, he states that the last genuine recorded sighting of the ghost, known as the Radiant Boy, was back in

venture out at night. Indeed, even during the daytime the good folk of this area would not dare to venture out alone; if they ventured out at all. Whitfield would frequent the area, frightening all and sundry, dominating, terrorising and stealing from the locals until one boy stood up to the tyrant. This brave lad put an end to Whitfield's activities, and, after his punishment was meted out, the people of Carlisle and the surrounding areas could sleep soundly once more, knowing that John Whitfield was now a rotting corpse.

Nowadays, you can hear the hum of car engines and trucks as they make their way up and down the nearby motorway, which now cuts through Barrock Park

Corby Castle, on the outskirts of the city, has one of the most well-known ghost accounts in the Carlisle area; that of the Radiant Boy.

Soon after we went to bed, we fell asleep; it might be between one and two in the morning when I awoke. I observed that the fire was totally extinguished; but although that was the case and we had no light, I saw a glimmer in the centre of the room which suddenly increased to a bright flame. I looked out, apprehending that something had caught fire; when, to my amazement, I beheld a beautiful boy, clothed in white, with bright locks resembling gold, standing by my bedside, in which position he remained some minutes, fixing his eyes upon me with a mild and benevolent expression. He then glided gently towards the other side of the chimney, where it is obvious there is no possible egress, and entirely disappeared. I found myself again in total darkness and all remained quiet until the usual hour of rising. I declare this to be a true account of what I saw at Corby Castle, upon my word as a clergyman.

1834. However, the ghost's most famous sighting occurred some years earlier than that, in the autumn of 1803. Hallam says that 'this is such a spectacular ghost of the last century that no book about the haunted north would be complete without telling it'; and I completely agree.

The Rector of Greystoke saw the ghost during a stay at the castle with his wife one night, resulting in their sharp exit from the castle after breakfast the following morning. His testimony reads as follows:

This amazing statement has been published and referred to many times over the years, and is by far the most well-known account of the phantom boy of Corby Castle. Interestingly, it is also said that there is a curse that goes with the sighting of the Radiant Boy, but that, one wonders, may only apply if you are one of the Howard clan. Apparently, should you encounter the ghost boy of Corby Castle it is said that you will, 'rise to fame for a while only then to be met by a violet or horrible death'. The Rector of Greystoke did not become famous, neither did he die horribly, subsequently living to a grand old age; perhaps, as he was only a guest at the castle, he was fortunate enough to escape the prophecy. It makes sense that this curse – for want of a better word – may indeed apply only to the Howards.

Dalston Hall Hotel

If you are looking for good ghosts stories in northern Cumbria then look no further than the beautiful Dalston Hall Hotel, near the village of Dalston. Located around three miles south of Carlisle, this wonderful hotel lays claim to a whole host of eerie phantoms and denizens of times gone by. The hotel is so haunted that it has attracted an abundance of interest from the paranormal community and has featured on a number of television programmes, such as GMTV and Living TV's *Most Haunted* (series 6). Newspapers (including the *Daily Mail*) have carried stories on the ghosts of Dalston Hall, and guests have often checked out of the hotel after their stay with some very strange stories to tell. Indeed, in a small pamphlet prepared by Dalston Hall and given to me by its current owner, the opening lines read:

The magnificent Dalston Hall.

As you drive through the quiet village of Dalston it is hard to imagine that this small community holds a deep dark secret… the spirits of Dalston Hall. As you open the heavy wooden front door and enter therein, the difference between the daylight outside, and the subdued dimness inside is truly notable; all around, the dark wood panelling makes the place intimate yet somewhat eerie.

The Dalston Crest. (Courtesy of Jan Mayer)

Before we take a look at the resident ghosts of Dalston we should take in its magnificent history. It is believed that when Cumberland was ceded to Scotland, David, King of the Scots gave the Manor of Little Dalston to his brother. We have it on the authority of a Dalston man that there is some evidence to support the following theory that the Dalston family begins with a certain Robert de Vallibus, brother of Hubert de Vallibus, the first Baron of Gilsland, by Robert de Meschines, Earl of Cumberland, who was granted the Manor in 1301. For the next 200 years the Dalstons appear to have been small landowners, taking part in the usual pastimes of the period, fighting the marauding Scots in border raids or undertaking garrison duties at Carlisle Castle. Gradually, they managed to increase the family fortunes. Records describing the building of Dalston Hall refer to the time when the first John Dalston dedicated the Pele Tower to his wife Elizabeth, whom he married in 1507. An inscription on an outside wall reads 'John Dalston Elizabeth mi wyf ys byldyng' – this has been written in Gothic script. The letters are all in reverse and can still be seen today.

At first, this tower stood alone. The first floor consisted of the usual vaulted chamber, originally the cellar and later becoming a chapel, which had the Ten Commandments painted on the walls; the spiral staircase was entered via an iron door and the two upper levels were a living room and a chamber respectively. Above this level was a fighting deck with battlements. From the time of John Dalston, the family held a powerful position in the counties of Cumberland and Westmorland, and in 1523 John Dalston's son, Thomas, was born. Soon after, their land possessions increased after purchasing from the Crown (Henry VIII) six Manors and various monastic lands, following the dissolution of the monasteries.

As the family fortunes increased, Dalston Hall was enlarged with buildings on the east of the Pele Tower and then on the west. When Thomas died in 1550, the family was held in some importance in the county and continued to be significant for the next 150 years. Thomas's son, Sir John Dalston, was born in 1523 and married Catherine Tolston of Bridekirk. Sir John became the Knight

The wooden stairwell that leads visitors to the haunted rooms and to the minstrel gallery, where one can get a spectacular view of the Baronial Hall.

Overlooking the Baronial Hall, this wooden door leads to the ancient stone tower steps that take you up to the bridal suite.

The stone staircase thought to be haunted by a lady who fell to her death.

last male of the family line. Lacking a male heir, he sold his estates at Dalston in 1761 (according to Daniel Defoe) to a Mr Monkhouse Davidson, grocer of London for £5,060. Dalston Hall had, by this time, been extended and the large hall added. In 1897, the hall and adjoining estates were purchased by Edmund Wright Stead, whose more recent restoration of this historic home earned the appreciation of antiquarian expert the late Canon Wilson, who wrote, 'Not one stone of interest was interfered with', and yet the result was 'a magnificent mansion surpassing perhaps even its ancient glories'. In later years, Dalston Hall was used as a Youth Training Centre, and in 1971 was converted into a hotel.

Old edifices, such as castles, stately homes and old halls, are always thought to be haunted, especially when there is so much history attached to the building, and Dalston Hall is no exception. It stands to reason that in the forty years or so of it being open to the public, something paranormal would have been seen, heard or sensed. If the stories are to be believed, then it most certainly has been. Some people suggest that there are six ghosts residing at the hotel, while others propose there are eight! The *Daily Mail*, when they ran their piece on the hotel, said there were only three ghosts, so whom do we believe? Well, at the end of the day it does not matter, as surely the fact that the hotel *is* haunted in the first place is the important thing. However, to obtain the finest information I could, rather than rely on untrustworthy internet sources – of which there are many – I decided to

of the Shire in 1556, and was also Sheriff in 1568 and 1578. James I knighted his son, yet another Sir John Dalston, and in 1592 he was commandant of the Citadel of Carlisle, which was a position of great trust.

Moving on through the years, Sir Charles Dalston (1686–1723), resided chiefly in Yorkshire and was Sheriff of Cumberland. Sir Charles had one son and six daughters and, accordingly, this one son, Sir George Dalston, was the

visit the hotel and talk to the hotel's staff and owner. If anyone will know about Dalston's ghosts, they will.

The owner, Jan Mayer, told me that just off the Baronial Hall an old wooden doorway opens up to a stone staircase. At the foot of these stairs there is an old iron gate, which dates back to the time when the hall was first built. At the back of the hotel two ancient towers are plain to see, and this old staircase spirals up to the top of the left tower. A little way up the stairwell there is a room that is built into the ancient tower and is now known as the honeymoon suite. Its walls are original stone and the windows are cut through blocks 3 feet thick. This tower is much older than the Baronial Hall, and dates from the early Middle Ages when it was the Pele Tower, which was put up as a defence against the Scots. The tower suite isn't actually noted to be haunted, Jan said, but on occasions guests have heard heavy footsteps on the tower steps outside the bedroom door. If you climb past this door on the stairwell you emerge onto the battlements at the top and, from there, if you look in a southerly direction, you will see the Cumbrian Fells. On a clear day this view is simply breathtaking.

The ghosts in this part of the hotel are reported to be a distressed female who, it is said, had thrown herself from the roof of the Pele Tower; some accounts suggest she actually fell down the aforementioned flight of stone stairs inside the tower and broke her neck. This spectre could well be responsible for the ghostly footfalls on the stairwell.

The bridal suite, which is located at the top of the ancient tower.

Room 4, one of the most haunted rooms at Dalston Hall.

Known as the ghost maid, another spectral visitor is said to haunt room 4 of the hotel. A member of staff who worked at Dalston Hall stayed in room 4 one night, and was rather disturbed to sense a presence, thought to be standing by the fireplace. They reported that whoever was there was standing quietly, as if they were watching this individual as they lay sleeping. Other people have also reported an odd sense of presence whilst sleeping in that room. Of course, there could be many explanations for this. Knowing

the room is allegedly haunted in the first place could go some way to account for the phenomenon. Being primed before entering allegedly haunted locations can induce certain expectations and when experiences are had, they can be ultimately deemed as paranormal ones. The fact that sleeping in a haunted hotel room – especially on your own – will no doubt also increase the adrenalin levels and consequently make you more nervous than usual. Being half asleep and actually dreaming spooky things is another good explanation. Having said that, one must keep an open mind and admit that there could well be a real ghost haunting room 4, making its presence known to the resident guests every now and again.

I was informed that another guest, who had been staying in the room, came down in the morning and asked to be relocated. She said she woke up to hear a dog snarling at the door. 'It kept growling intermittently all night,' she said, 'though there was nothing to be seen'. In 1996, another guest awoke to find a lady sitting on the bed next to him. The ghost spoke to him but her voice seemed to come from behind him, and not from her actual mouth. Afterwards, he couldn't remember a word that she had said to him, and he mentioned that he hadn't been frightened at all during the experience. There is, apparently, a second ghost said to inhabit room 4 at the Dalston Hall Hotel and she is known as Emily. Her ghost is said to stand by the window and gaze out, whilst at the same time nervously playing with a ring she has upon her finger. Some folk suggest that this ring could be an engagement ring from her beloved, and therefore the assumption is that she could be yearning for him to return from wherever it was he went. Another phenomena that has been reported in this room includes the sightings of strange anthropomorphic shapes seen in the peripheral vision; noises similar to that of something heavy being dragged across a wooden floor, even though all the floors are carpeted; and, most harrowingly, the eerie sound of laughter heard reverberating around the room.

The next ghost of Dalston Hall is said to be the property's oldest ghost and is said to haunt the gallery above the Baronial Hall. She is the classic 'grey lady' ghost. I have lost count of the amount of grey ladies I have investigated over the years, and it seems that wherever you go, a grey lady awaits you! This grey lady, who is thought to date back to the Tudor times, is known as 'Lady Jane' – a name given to her by the hotel staff – and is said to walk quietly along the minstrel's gallery. She is thought to have been a member of the Dalston family that once resided here, although

The Baronial Hall. The ghost here is thought to date back to Tudor times and is known as Lady Jane – a name given to her by the hotel staff – and is said to walk quietly along the minstrel's gallery.

which one exactly, no one knows. There is also a spectral handyman or caretaker that is said to date back to around the time of Queen Victoria. He is said to haunt the cellar areas. Others suggest he also haunts the hotel grounds. There is a story that states the ghost of the handyman had been seen in the cellar; it was even reported that he has actually handed tools to another workman who had been carrying out work down there. This, Jan Mayer told me, was in the 1960s. The phantom handyman is described as being a big burly fellow, who wears tweed trousers.

Interestingly, more than one of the hotel's porters, has heard noises from down in the cellars when making their rounds in the dead of the night. They have all described the sounds of wooden barrels being handled and rolled around. But, wooden barrels have not been used for many years in Dalston Hall. In 1997, the noises were once again heard and one brave soul actually went down to investigate them. He said he saw the figure of a man, but lost his nerve and turned back to come out. He then asked the girl on the desk who the man was, but the receptionist told him he must have been mistaken as there was no one else down there at that time.

Room 12, it seems, is also a haunted room. Many people who have slept in this room over the years have complained of being woken up in the night by girl's voices whispering, although no one has reported anything unpleasant happening, yet. Those lucky enough to hear these voices always say that they just seem to be having a good time; the trouble is that nobody is ever actually there. Back

in October 1996, candles that were used for medieval banquets in the Baronial Hall were seen by staff to flare up by themselves. During the same month, glasses were also heard to smash in empty rooms, and upon inspection were found broken a good distance from the shelves they had been stacked on; pint glasses rose into the air on their own; the library windows were once found flung open, and the night porter reported the sound of planks banging together. In October 1997, the telephone system went haywire, when all the phones began ringing. When they were answered there was no one there, yet they kept ringing every ten minutes until this strange phenomenon stopped as mysteriously as it had begun. Lights were also reported to have flickered on and off, along with the fire alarm system reporting fires that had not actually occurred.

So there you have it; Dalston's most popular and well known ghost tales. But there are more, it seems. After visiting the hotel again in the summer of 2011, and speaking to a few more of its staff members to try and ascertain further data, they informed me that 'when it comes to ghosts there are indeed plenty at Dalston, allegedly'. I like their use of the word 'allegedly', which tells me that although they are open-minded about the possibility of the existence of ghosts, they are not altogether convinced they are, in actual fact, real. This also tells me that Dalston Hall's business is not drummed up by the 'haunted hotel' angle. Indeed, the lack of information regarding ghosts on their actual website also supports this fact. The pamphlet I referred to earlier onwas designed for those who show an interest in ghosts and for those who specifically ask about them, as I did.

This concludes this section on the Dalston Hall Hotel and its ghosts, and I offer my sincere thanks to the hotel's owner, Jan, and the staff members for sharing these amazing stories with me, and for allowing me to print the information detailing the resident ghosts, and the history of this magnificent hotel.

The Ghosts of Talkin Tarn, Near Brampton

Talkin Tarn Country Park has been run by Carlisle City Council since 2006. This beautiful 165-acre site encompasses mature woodland, lush meadows, and a large glacial tarn, which is one of the main attractions here. Talkin Tarn, by all accounts, was used rather a lot by the Victorians and many people came from Brampton and Carlisle to spend time here; many people still do. With an abundance of wildlife, remarkable scenery, and acres of paths and trails for the avid rambler, Talkin Tarn is a place which will no doubt attract people for many years to come. The first of the ghosts of Talkin Tarn – for it is said that it is haunted by a number of them – is thought to date from the Victorian era, after a woman called Jessie allegedly drowned in the lake back in 1850.

Apparently, she was murdered there after explaining to her lover that she was going to reveal their illicit love affair to everyone. Quite often the couple would meet up after dark and make love down by the tarn; it was a night-time rendezvous that both parties enjoyed,

until Jessie explained her plans. This could not happen as Jessie's lover was already engaged to a wealthy landowner's daughter from Carlisle, something that Jessie knew nothing about. After attempting to bribe her with money, which she declined, her lover decided he had to kill her to keep her quiet. So, after having sex with her down by the water's edge for one last time, he dragged her into the tarn, held her head under the water and drowned her. After killing her so ruthlessly, he disposed of her body by dumping it in the lake. Her sad, confused ghost is said to forever haunt the lakeside of Talkin Tarn, wondering just why her lover decided to take her life.

A better-known ghost, however, goes by the title of 'Old Martha, the old woman of Talkin Tarn'. There are many versions of this story so it must be specified that the following account is merely my take on the tale. Martha was said to have been one of the village's oldest residents. She spoke to no one and kept herself to herself, which in those days was not the thing to do. Gossip was aplenty and poor old Martha was always at the brunt of their idle chit-chat. She had no family and never had visitors. Children were afraid of her because of the vicious rumours and they never dared to venture near her home in case she somehow caused them some harm. One day, people noticed that she looked rather odd. She appeared ill, with her neck and face covered in an awful looking angry red rash, which seemed to swell to a noticeable degree. Not many people offered to help her, and those that did were turned away; she was, it seems, a proud woman.

Talkin Tarn on the outskirts of Carlisle. An old village is said to lie deep beneath the murky depths, and rumours persist that the area is haunted by a woman called Jessie who was murdered here in 1850.

Over the next few days, the only time Martha was spotted was when she was making her way to and from the village spring, where she collected her water. This spring, which led to the local pond, was the main water supply to the village and was used by all residents there. After a week or so, her appearance seemed to be getting better and she became more active. The swelling on her neck and face disappeared but it left rather ugly looking scars and blotches all over, leaving her horribly disfigured.

Soon after Martha made her recovery, the local children began to come down with the same symptoms that Martha suffered the previous week. Swelling of the face and neck, fever, and sickness soon took hold and, sadly, most of the infected children were soon dead, unable to handle this plague–like disease. Nowadays, it would be plain to see that the local pond, which was used for washing the animals, was obviously contaminated by some kind of disease and therefore using the water to drink and wash with was not ideal. However, when the townsfolk began to drop like flies, another explanation was sought. They began to suspect foul play and blamed it on the work of the devil, or, more conveniently, someone in cahoots with the devil. Because Martha had survived the disease, and was already seen as the local witch, she was easy pickings for the villagers. It was decided that she that was in league with Satan and that something had to be done.

The following day, on her next trip to the fresh water spring, she was accosted by a horde of irate villagers, who demanded to know just how, and why, she brought disaster and death upon their little village. When confronted by the villagers, Martha was very afraid to say the least. She tried to escape and make her way back to her cottage, but one of the villagers picked up a large brick and threw it at her. It hit her quite hard on the torso and made her stumble. Then, another stone came and hit her again, and in her panic she tripped and fell straight into the dirty pond. As she came up to the surface she uttered the words, 'Water, water, you must use the clean water'. Old Martha was using the source of water at the top of the hill, which was clean, unlike the water that was contaminated in the pond below, which the villagers were sharing with their animals. The villagers realised this and presumed she was using the clean source of water because she knew that the pond was infected; they took this as a sign that she had infected the village's water supply. They continued to 'brick' her until she disappeared for good under the bloodstained surface of the pond. As she sunk under for the final time, the words, 'Water, clean water' were heard once more. The villagers fell silent,

knowing they had done wrong. They looked at one another and then began to try to and convince each other that they had done a good deed, 'Martha was a witch, she killed our children,' they murmured to themselves. They eventually returned to their own homes, convinced that they had done what was needed to be done.

That night it began to rain. The rain lashed down upon the village like it had never rained before and it was rather unnerving to say the least. The village became muddy and eventually so waterlogged that no one would venture outside. The rain, it seemed, was never going to stop. Originally, there was only one spring that fed water into the pond, but now there were at least half a dozen. They had come from nowhere and the level of the water was still rising; a cause for concern for the villagers. Soon, the houses that stood close to the pond were completely flooded and by now well abandoned. A few days later it was still raining and all the villagers had rounded up what belongings they could and left the village, which just happened to be in a deep valley. It was eventually flooded to the point where it was now completely submerged and lost forever; a new tarn taking its place. The people who had managed to escape the flooding began building new homes on higher ground, and these homes were apparently the beginning of the present day Talkin village.

It is said that if you visit the area known as Talkin Tarn at the right time of year, namely the anniversary of this event, you can hear the faint sound of Martha's voice still warning people not to drink the infected water supply. 'Clean water, more water...clean water, more water...clean water, more water...' until the sound of the tarn itself drowns it out, just as it did with the old village many, many years ago. It seems Talkin Tarn could really be a 'talking tarn' if you believe the legend. It is also thought that on midsummer's day – if you listen carefully enough – you will also hear the eerie chimes of the bells ringing out from the submerged school, calling the ghost children to their classes.

The Blacksmiths Arms Pub, Talkin

According to Alan Robson in his book, *Grisly Trails and Ghostly Tales* (Virgin Books, 1992) the Blacksmith's Arms Pub in the village of Talkin is haunted by a former landlady called Maggie, who was known to have been a lot tougher than the average male, and was renowned for not taking any prisoners, so to speak – a landlady not to be messed with. When ghostly things began to occur in the old pub – long after Maggie's time there, which was in the early 1900s – the locals believed it was her 'up to her tricks again', and even though week after week the paranormal activity occurred in the little old inn, the locals were not phased about it in the least.

Another ghost is also said to haunt this pub, however, and she is known as the ghost of Mary Stobbart. Trying to gather information regarding this particular ghost proved to be rather difficult, and I was only able to find one reference

to her, anywhere; and that yielded very little in the way of information. I then contacted the pub directly and asked the present owners if there was anything in this story. I was informed that although a story was attached to the pub regarding a ghost, the present owners did not believe a word of it and I was asked not to tell the story of Mary Stobbart; so I won't.

The Wizard of Carrock Fell

Carrock Fell lies in the far north of the picturesque English Lake District, and even its name conjures up visions of its ancient position within the topography of the landscape. The word carrock has its origin in the old Welsh word *carrec*, or *carrac*, from which some say we also receive the English word 'crag'. It basically means 'stone' or 'rock'. The word 'fell' derives from the old Viking word *fjall*, which means 'mountain'. Carrock Fell, then, simply means 'stony mountain', which seems to be a case of stating the obvious, but it isn't; it is littered with thousands of slate-grey rocks and boulders which give a truly startling appearance. It is a breathtakingly beautiful place which lies not far from the outskirts of Carlisle.

Now, the beauty of Carrock Fell is not its only attraction, particularly if you are interested in hauntings or indeed any other kind of preternatural phenomena. There is, it must be said, something truly odd about it. First, though, we need to acquaint ourselves with the history of Carrock Fell, for it has a long and ancient one.

There once stood an oval-shaped Iron Age hill fort on top of the fell, which, from a military point of view, enjoyed significant strategic advantages. It was erected by one of the Celtic tribes and was truly sturdy. But then, alas, the soldiers of Rome arrived and the fort's occupiers discovered, to their cost, the military sophistication and might of Rome, where enemies – even in well-defended and poorly accessible hill forts – could simply be swept to one side. Soon, only paltry vestiges of the fort remained; a few stones, in fact. And time, seizing the opportunity, began to weather them away.

In the thirteenth century, a man called Michael Scot gained a legendary reputation as a wizard, which stretched throughout Europe; his name being whispered in hushed tones due to the authority he commanded and the reverence he was shown. Scot's abilities were, by tradition, nothing short of awesome. He is said to have built, to the amazement of locals, a church in the space of a single night. Even the famous Long Meg stone circle was believed to be his creation, for it is said that he came across a coven of witches on that spot and turned them all to stone.

He was a competent astronomer and it is claimed that he was able to measure the distance between the earth and the stars, something that was simply impossible in his day. He also had a reputation as a healer and was said to have healed a Roman Emperor of a serious ailment, although the authenticity of this story is extremely doubtful. If the incident did take place, then the person whom Scot healed was likely to have been Pope Honorius III, who held Scot in high regard after the wizard was ordained as a Roman Catholic priest and became a monk. In stark contrast to the teachings of the Church, Scot was said to be able to control the tides of the sea by a mere sweep of his hand and summon up demons to do his bidding through the use of arcane rites. After his death, his voluminous writings were taken to Wolsty Castle in Cumbria.

Among the many other feats attributed to Michael Scot was the appearance of the incredible number of stones that can still be seen at Carrock Fell to this day. It is said that he threw them there, single-handedly, by virtue of his magical powers. His ghost is, quite predictably, said to haunt the area to this day, which perhaps explains why the Fell is sometimes referred to as 'Old Nick's Fell', or, if you like, the Devil's Mountain.

In 1857, novelists Charles Dickens and Wilkie Collins climbed up the mount to Carrock Fell. Dickens described it as a cold, windswept place. However, the two authors did examine the remains of a building which was said to be Scot's house. Scot, of course, was the builder; or, according to some, the Devil himself. Despite its dilapidation, Dickens stated that it was still 'spectacular'. Perhaps the ghost of the enigmatic and inscrutable Michael Scot still resides there; who knows?

Afterword

I must say in the first instance that writing *Haunted Carlisle* has been an absolute pleasure. At the beginning of this book project I honestly thought I may have struggled to reach the word limit required from the publisher, but as I made my trips time and time again across the top of England to explore this wonderful ancient city, and the areas surrounding it, I soon realised that not only was I going to reach the limit that was required of me, but exceed it. Wherever I roamed in my search for tales of the supernatural in Carlisle, I found myself discovering new and unknown (at least to me) tales of ghosts, phantoms and spirits.

During my time in Carlisle I have met some of the most wonderful, kind and friendly people one could ever wish to come across, and have made some good friends along the way. I have drank beer in pubs, eaten tea and scones in coffee shops, taken tours of hotels, railway stations and castles in my quest for unearthing the ghosts of Carlisle, and I have to say, hand on heart, it has

Abbey Street is one of the many old-world areas of Carlisle that helps to give the region its charm and character.

been a truly magnificent experience. I have learned so much about Carlisle's haunted heritage since undertaking this project, and I am so pleased about this. I knew Carlisle had ghosts but I never knew there were so many! Carlisle, at least in my eyes, has so much in common with my hometown, Newcastle-upon-Tyne, and I feel that writing this book has given me a bond with this city that I will never lose.

Like Newcastle, it is a former walled-town with a host of ancient cobbled paths, alleyways, and nooks and crannies all begging to be explored. Ancient edifices are in abundance, standing proudly alongside newer modern buildings, with ghosts residing everywhere. Both cities stand proud at the gates of England and both are united by Hadrian's magnificent Roman wall. Carlisle and Newcastle have a lot more in common than I ever realised.

May I finally say that I sincerely hope that you, the reader, have enjoyed my efforts to enlighten you regarding the phantoms and apparitions, as well as the paranormal history of this fascinating place, as much as I have enjoyed visiting and researching them.

About the Author

DARREN W. Ritson is a ghost hunter and paranormal investigator who was born in Newcastle-upon-Tyne and now lives in North Tyneside with his partner, Jayne Watson, and their daughter Abbey May Ritson. He took an interest in paranormal matters at an early age after experiencing poltergeist activity in France in 1986. Darren is the founding member of the well-known North East Ghost Research Team, which often features in the media. In 2005, he co-founded the Ghosts and Hauntings Overnight Surveillance Team, and in 2007 co-founded WraithScape – Paranormal with a Passion. Darren has carried out over 150 overnight paranormal investigations in over 100 different locations and, with Mike Hallowell, documented one of the most vicious and intense poltergeist cases on record – the South Shields poltergeist. In 2006, Darren joined the Incorporated Society for Psychical Research (SPR) and now corresponds with some of the world's finest investigators. These include the legendary Colin Wilson, Guy Lyon Playfair, Peter Underwood FSRA, and Alan Murdie. Darren has travelled the country lecturing on poltergeist phenomena, and has been invited to conduct talks with some of the leading academic research associations into psychic study, including the Incorporated Society for Psychical Research (SPR), the Ghost Club of Great Britain, and the Scottish Society for Psychical Research (SSPR). Darren has also lectured on ghosts and poltergeists at Northumbria University after receiving a request from Dr Nick Neave (Head of Psychology/Parapsychology).

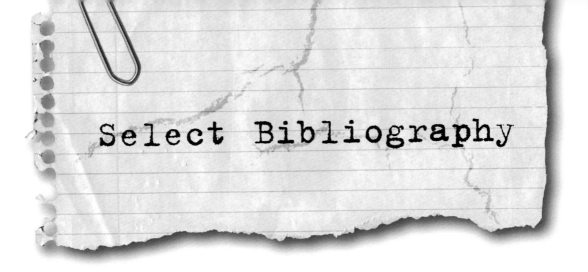

Select Bibliography

Books

Day, James Wentworth, *In Search of Ghosts* (Muller, 1969)

Haining, Peter, *Ghosts,* (BCA, 1974)

Hallum, Jack, *Ghosts of the North* (David & Charles, 1976)

Hapgood, Sarah, *500 British Ghosts and Hauntings* (Foulsham, 1993)

Harries, John, *The Ghost Hunters Road Book* (Letts, 1968)

Hippisley Coxe, Antony D., *Haunted Britain* (Pan, 1973)

Kirkup, Rob, *Ghostly Northumbria* (The History Press, 2008)

Lyndon Dodds, Glen, *Historic Sites of Northumberland and Newcastle-upon-Tyne* (Albion Press, 2002)

MacKenzie, Andrew, *Hauntings and Apparitions* (Heinemann, 1982)

Maple, Eric, *Supernatural England* (Hale, 1977)

O'Donnell, Elliot, *Haunted Britain* (Rider, 1948)

Poole, Keith B., *Haunted Heritage* (Guild Publishing, 1988)

Price, Harry, *Poltergeist over England* (Country Life Ltd, 1945)

Puttick, Betty, *Supernatural England* (Countryside Books, 2002)

Ritson, Darren W., *Haunted Newcastle* (The History Press, 2009)

Ibid., *Ghost Hunter: True Life Encounters from the North East* (GHP, 2006)

Ibid., Darren W., *In Search of Ghosts: Real Hauntings from Around Britain* (Amberley, 2008)

Ibid., *Supernatural North* (Amberley, 2009)

Ibid., *Ghosts at Christmas* (The History Press, 2010)

Robson, Alan, *Grisly Trails and Ghostly Tales* (Virgin Books, 1992)

Underwood, Peter, *This Haunted Isle* (Harrap, 1984)

Ibid., *A Gazetteer or British Ghosts* (Souvenir Press, 1971)

Ibid., *A-Z of British Ghosts* (Souvenir Press, 1971)

Websites

www.newsandstar.co.uk
www.cumberlandnews.co.uk
www.bbc.co.uk
www.borderreivers.org.uk
www.dailymail.co.uk
www.carlisleshistory.co.uk
nli.northampton.ac.uk
en.wikipedia.org
www.carlisleundercroft.co.uk
www.cumberlandnews.co.uk

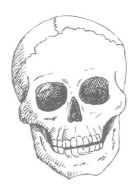

If you enjoyed this book, you may also be interested in …

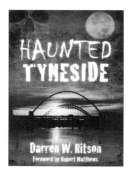

Haunted Tyneside
DARREN W. RITSON

This book contains a terrifying collection of true-life, spine-chilling tales from across Tyneside. Featuring stories of unexplained phenomena, apparitions and poltergeists, including the phantom monk of Tynemouth Priory, the restless spirit of Newcastle's Jin Jameson, the haunting of Willington Mill and the notorious South Shields Poltergeist case. This book is guaranteed to make your blood run cold.

978 0 7524 5824 3

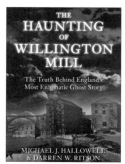

The Haunting of Willington Mill:
The Truth Behind England's Most Enigmatic Ghost Story
MICHAEL J. HALLOWELL & DARREN W. RITSON

During the nineteenth century Willington Mill, near Wallsend, gained an infamous reputation for being haunted. The case attracted the interest of the country's leading psychical researchers of the time, but the mystery was never solved – until now. Michael J. Hallowell and Darren W. Ritson have pieced together the true story of Willington Mill, detailing the fascinating phenomena that occurred in the building.

978 0 7524 5878 6

Murder & Crime Northumberland
PAUL HESLOP

Spanning a period of nearly 100 years, this book opens with the killing of Thomas Hamilton, whose body was discovered lying at the foot of the town's walls at Berwick-upon-Tweed. Also included here is the case of John Dickman, hanged for shooting a man on the railway, and Albert Edward Matheson, who murdered 15-year-old Gordon Lockhart. With a wide selection of sources and illustrated with more than fifty images this collection will appeal to everyone interested in true crime and the shadier side of Northumberland's past.

978 0 7524 5872 4

The South Shields Poltergeist:
One Family's Fight Against An Invisible Intruder
MICHAEL J. HALLOWELL & DARREN W. RITSON

This is a truly terrifying account which details the authors' struggle with an invisible, malicious entity that threatened and intimidated anyone who dared to stand up to it. A man had his torso slashed; knives, coins and other objects were thrown around, and children's toys spoke to the investigators. The book is based on the testimonies of those who actually experienced the South Shields Poltergeist at first hand.

978 0 7524 5274 6

Visit our website and discover thousands of other History Press books.

www.thehistorypress.co.uk